127105

D0336992

13.31   Cw 10/13

Child-Initiated Learning

Positive Relationships in the Early Years

by Jennie Lindon

Updated to reflect the 2012 EYFS

Children's interests at

What does child-initiated

What does adult-led me

A balance between chil

What is meant by indivi

The role of the early y

Being a partner in play

The emotional environm

Communicative adults:

What is 'sustained sha

Leading a child-foc

Planning that pays off

Promoting active first-l

Observation to work a

A welcoming learning

Respect for physically

Published by Practical Pre-School Books, A Division of MA Education Ltd, St Jude's Church, Dulwich Road, Herne Hill, London, SE24 0PB.
Tel: 020 7738 5454 www.practicalpreschoolbooks.com

© MA Education Ltd 2010. Revised edition 2013. Illustrations by Cathy Hughes. Front cover image photo taken by Lucie Carlier © MA Education Ltd.

ISBN 978-1-909280-20-5

Children's interests at the heart of learning

Young children have only one go at their early childhood.

- They should emerge with a store of treasured memories and secure that they really matter to a small number of adults, with whom they have spent their time.

- Adults are responsible for cherishing young children, ensuring that they feel liked for who they are and competent within their own world.

- Children need an early childhood in which they have plenty of time to explore, alongside adults who respect young children's interests and how they learn.

Best practice over the long history of early years provision has been that: days for young children should be full of opportunities for children to learn within a nurturing environment, through their self-chosen play and with generous time outdoors. The role of supporting adults is: to protect that time, provide suitable resources and be a friendly play and conversational partner, whilst taking good care of the physical and emotional needs of babies and young children. Genuinely helpful early years practitioners – and parents too – need to have realistic expectations based on a close relationship with this individual baby or child, as well as a sound basis of child development knowledge in general.

In their different ways, the early years frameworks which apply to each part of the UK support this perspective on early childhood. However, the Early Years Foundation Stage (EYFS) in England is the only Birth to Five framework within the UK. Wales and Northern Ireland start with three-year-olds and Scotland has an under-threes framework separate from the 3-17 Curriculum for Excellence. The ideas that follow in this book are relevant to early years provision across the UK, but the cross-referencing is mainly to the EYFS.

What does child-initiated mean?

The first edition of the EYFS (2007) created a strong focus on the importance of child-initiated learning through children's active choice about what to do within any day. The role of early years practitioners is that of supporting young children to learn at their own pace and in ways that make sense to them.

The recently revised EYFS (DfE, 2012) has confirmed this essential approach in section 1.9. This part of the statutory framework reaffirms the importance of play and a balanced mix of adult-led and child-initiated activity. A key sentence is that: 'Children learn by leading their own play, and by taking part in play which is guided by adults'. The Welsh Foundation Phase framework (2008) has a similar focus on children's ability to choose freely from a range of activities. Adult input is valuable, but only when the approach to planning is flexible.

So what does the phrase 'child-initiated' actually mean? In my dictionary, the word 'initiate' is defined as to 'begin, commence, enter upon, to introduce, set going, originate'. So, child-initiated activities and experiences are those which babies or children have indicated they want to do and in this way. The children are the originators; they set this current activity going from what is available to them. Through their personal choice, young children – including babies and young toddlers – are busy directing their own learning.

They can do something that is interesting or exciting to them and then repeat immediately, if they wish. They can practise those skills they are motivated to improve. They explore through actions and their powers of communication, using what they want to show or ask you. The phrase child-initiated learning can only make sense when children have plenty of scope to decide what deserves their time and full attention on any given day.

Practice Guidance

The first edition of the EYFS did not explain what was meant by the terms child-initiated or adult-led. This was a regrettable oversight, given that a serious problem had been created in recent years because a primary school definition of child-initiated had infiltrated early years practice. This primary-based approach promoted the view that activities could be judged as child-initiated, when an adult had pre-determined most of the details of the experience before young children ever got their hands and eyes on any resources. Within the more structured primary school day these timetabled sections of the day might also be called independent learning times. More accurately, they are times when children are able to remain focused on a selected array of resources without the presence of a guiding adult. This working definition of child-initiated continues to appear in some practical materials written for early years practitioners.

This misguided perspective – for early childhood – was supported over the same period by the imposition of an outcomes-led lesson plan approach. This view depended on the bizarre idea that it was actually possible to design and run activities for young children that would assuredly deliver specific learning outcomes. Such a developmentally unsound notion creaked around the edges when applied to the eldest children within the early childhood age range. It progressively cracked when applied to three- or four-year-olds and shattered when practitioners tried to apply inflexible, pre-planned activities to toddlers and babies.

Fortunately, the second edition of the EYFS (in 2008) added a new section to the Practice Guidance booklet on page 7. It was made very clear that child-initiated activities are self-chosen from a well-resourced learning environment, for instance that a child decides to play with the fire engine and determines how that play unfolds in detail. A further example given was that a child brings an item into their early years setting, or talks about an experience from family life. Early years practitioners then support this expressed interest with relevant resources. It was also made clear that children may initiate their own choices by taking ownership of an adult-initiated activity. The example given was of a child choosing to pour water into a hole to create a puddle, rather than water the plants as the adult had envisaged.

Best early years practice is full of young children, busy following their own enterprises, fully supported by equally interested adults. This book is resourced by examples I gained easily from my visits to the settings thanked on page 38. Those visits were usually one day only; the longest was two days. Here is the first example to begin the process of sharing what child-initiated learning looks like for real children in actual provision. Please look for echoes of your own good practice in this description.

Look closer: The drummers who became plumbers

An absorbing child-initiated experience (stretched to 40 minutes) on my visit to Kennet Day Nursery started when three boys selected large kitchen implements which were in the large tray for scooping pasta. The children started to use them for drumming and tapping on the outdoor equipment. This choice meant that there were no more implements in the pasta, so one practitioner suggested: "Shall we go and find some sticks inside. I'm sure we have some". The children came back with handfuls of sticks – some wooden chopsticks and some long paintbrushes, which they held by the brush end.

Five children, four boys and one girl started to drum on the fixed outdoor cylinders that reverberated like drums. The children used different techniques: using one stick, two sticks and then one boy tapped one stick onto his other stick and told the practitioner: "That's what real drummers do". One boy started to tap two drum cylinders at the same time. A girl was experimenting with tapping the metal bars of the bridge structure of their outdoor climbing equipment.

Another practitioner joined the children and began to experiment with his own rhythm, also using two chopsticks. He did not suggest that the children – now three boys – copy him; he was playing alongside. But they chose to imitate some of the rhythmic patterns that the adult had created. He and the boys continued to drum together in companionable sound making, sometimes keeping very close to a shared beat. After some time, this practitioner moved to join the girl who was still experimenting with tapping the metal bars of the bridge.

We're fixing the pipes, because the water is stuck in there, and we're going to get it out.

I'm going to get these screws out to fix the pipe!

When I next looked, the boy drummers had moved across to the other side of the garden and, accompanied by other boys, were now on their knees in a line where the firm surface joined the earth. Everyone was single-mindedly digging at the very edge of the garden with their chopsticks. The practitioner who was with the drummers at the outset was sitting and watching the boys. Her open-ended question about what was happening brought the reply: "We're fixing the pipes, because the water's stuck in there and we're going to get it out". Chopsticks were now being used as tools to make holes in the earth. One boy was twisting his chopstick and explained: "I'm going to get these screws out to fix the pipe".

The conversation and the hard digging work continued for another 15 minutes or so. There was conversation between the children – in the end a team of six plumbers, including one girl. Two practitioners were close by, one of whom was digging with the children. The plumbers were sure that they had to find the pipes, which at one point became cables, and that it was definitely not a good idea for water to get stuck. There was some discussion around what they would have to do when they finally reached the pipes.

One of the practitioners explained afterwards to me that the nursery had been flooded recently due to water overflowing, and one family had experienced a similar problem at home. Either of these events could have been behind the pretend play sequence.

What does adult-led mean?

Child-initiated experiences are not better than adult-led – no more than activities organised by adults are of a higher quality than those initiated by the children. The two broad types work in different ways, which is the reason why the revised EYFS continues to direct practitioners to create a balance between the two. Effective early years practitioners understand the difference and how, within a suitably flexible day, there is not a firm division between child-initiated and adult-led, but rather a flexible to-and-fro.

The 2008 edition of the EYFS Practice Guidance provided a descriptive explanation of what was meant by adult-led activities. The essence of this broad type of event is that the adult has selected this time to encourage a specific aspect of learning or to discuss something in particular. The practitioner takes a leading role, which still leaves significant scope for children to influence what happens this time, let alone what will follow on from an adult idea that the children judge to be a good one. An adult-led activity could also be a small group time, but in the Practice Guidance this descriptive option was just an example. You could definitely take an adult lead, possibly briefly, without your action being part of an activity you planned earlier.

In no version of the EYFS has there ever been a requirement for a given number of group times in a day – and this kind of event is unsuitable for any under-threes. Certainly there is no direction that adult-led activity means the same as circle time or other forms of getting young children together in a group in which there is a need for listening as well as talking. Older threes and fours may respond well to a conversational small group time. It is reasonable to say that such a group time gets no larger than the guiding adult could easily stretch out and touch each child. If the group gets much larger than this size, you will not hold the attention of those young children who cannot get close to you.

Look closer: Playing the board game

In Start Point Sholing, a practitioner was playing a simple board game with Harry (four years). They had a large die with either one or two dots on each side. The aim of the game was to move around the supermarket board, picking up items of (pretend) fruit and vegetables from the spaces and adding them to your own little basket. This activity is a good example of an adult as a supportive play partner, enabling children to engage in a chosen activity, which is unlikely to be possible without the adult.

The pair were joined by Ben (three years), who asked to play. Ben and Harry were very focused: taking turns to throw the die, identifying the one or two dots, counting their moves on the board and working out if they had, or had not, gained a piece of fruit or vegetable this time. The practitioner also took part in the game and he was ready to help Ben, who was a less confident counter. The two children, out of choice, usually repeated the name of the food they had gained for their basket.

The boys wanted another go and then a third boy arrived and asked to join. The three boys played another full game, with the practitioner focused on showing the new player how the game worked. He continued to support the play discretely: guiding with, "Can you pass the dice to Ben, please", confirming that the throw was one or two and guiding, if necessary, the direction of counting to move the pieces. Sometimes he helped the boys to anticipate the play with, "If you get one, you'll get the onion. If you get two…".

Practitioners may introduce children to a particular material, skill or idea. Then, over time, direct adult help will be needed less, because children become adept at this skill or area of knowledge and can operate independently. By the nature of learning, they will appreciate your help and guidance with a skill or area of knowledge that is currently more of a puzzle. You continue to be important to young boys and girls. However, when you have a sustained relationship with children over time, you experience continual change over those enterprises in which they want your full and direct help or just a bit of assistance. Sometimes children want you as an admiring companion who responds swiftly to "Look, look!". In my visits I observed a great deal of this evidence of a strong relationship between children and familiar adults. Young children acted so as to engage practitioners and looked confident that, of course, the adults would be just as interested or excited.

If you get 'one', you'll get the onion.

Young children cannot ask to do something again, like go to the market, until they have done it at least once before. There are many valuable experiences that will not be available to young children without some prior organisation and guidance from a familiar adult. Young children will enjoy some of these first-time-around experiences with you in their early years provision. However, some valuable experiences will travel in with children from their family time. Older twos and over-threes will often tell you about interesting times from their home life. Continued and open communication with parents is the vital channel when babies and very young children cannot share their experiences in words.

The EYFS statutory framework does not use the term 'adult-initiated', and does not really acknowledge 'child-led', although both concepts are present in guidance materials that have been published since 2007. If the aim is to distinguish the different ways of approaching experiences for young children, you might as well do a thorough job on the options.

- Adults cannot lead an activity without initiating it – starting the process, setting off a train of thought or hands-on exploration

- Any adult-led activity should have emerged from your knowledge of the children with whom you spend your days. Your good ideas – and definitely any book, article or online activity resource – must tuck in behind alert observation of what currently interests children. You can only lead in a sensible way by following the interests of these babies or children.

- Adult-led activities may be those which include a small group of children in a focussed, shared conversation about something of direct interest. However, adult-led experiences are not exclusively about a group time, scheduled or not.

- Thoughtful practitioners and teams also consider what kind of shared group time works for young children and when is the most sensible timing within a day or session. The settings described in this book use key person time as the main or only small group time in the day or session – more about those experiences in Lindon (2010).

- Within early childhood, up to and including the reception year, any adult-led or initiated activity should have plenty of scope for children to influence the direction of the activity. Any plans for key group time need to be open-ended and any small group circle time should not be planned down to the last detail.

Links to your practice

Despite the explanation in the second edition of the EYFS (2008), some confusion has continued over what exactly is covered by the term 'child-initiated'. One issue raised, in some internet forum strands is: how can young children truly initiate any activity, because an adult has always done something? Is this a question for you, or something that puzzles your team?

The answer is, of course, that young children can only begin a chosen enterprise with the available resources and within their learning environment, which adults determine. Toddlers cannot embark on a sustained exploration of what you can do with a large cardboard box, if nobody gives them this kind of open-ended resource. Adults are also crucial because they organise the timing and flow of a day that welcomes young children to pursue their consuming interest in how you run a garage, real and pretend, and to initiate spontaneous conversations.

Child-initiated experiences have been freely chosen by individual children or small groups of friends. The adult role is to come alongside as a friendly play companion, a partner in conversation or sometimes just as an interesting onlooker, who is learning from this informal observation.

A balance between child-initiated and adult-led

The EYFS (DfE, 2012, paragraph 1.9) promotes a balance between child-initiated and adult-led activities, whilst leaving early years practitioners to make an ongoing judgement about the appropriate proportion within a day or week. It is useful to go back to the

Effective Provision of Pre-school Education (EPPE) research. The EPPE project was a major source of these ideas within the 2007 EYFS materials. The main messages of the EPPE project were:

- The most effective early years settings – in terms of children's learning – had a balance of about two-thirds child-initiated experiences to one-third adult-initiated activities.

- The EPPE team use the term child-initiated with the same meaning given earlier in this section and the reports use the phrase 'freely chosen'.

- The best provision – and the research observations were only undertaken in group settings – had a pattern in which practitioners came alongside children in about half of those child-initiated experiences.

- The EPPE team (in reports and presentations) are clear that the exact proportion is less important than how practitioners actually behave when they are with young children. Adult actions and communicative interaction make the difference for children within child – and adult-initiated experiences – rather than achieving a magic number of different types of activities.

- However, the developmentally appropriate balance, from the EPPE research data, is definitely tipped towards more child-initiated than adult-initiated activities within a day or session.

- This stronger focus on children's self-chosen enterprises, in contrast with activities pre-planned by the adults, was clearly stated within the EYFS materials. This balance was also reflected in the requirement to weight any observations, up to and including the content of the Early Years Foundation Stage Profile (EYFSP), towards children's self-chosen play and conversations. The revised EYFS (DfE, 2012) is less detailed but still stresses ongoing observations.

- The EPPE research did not include observations of children younger than two years of age and the majority were of three- to five-year-olds. The team recognised that some reception class teams struggled to maintain a suitable balance for young children between child-initiated and adult-initiated experiences.

Reports from the EPPE project, for instance Siraj-Blatchford et al (2002), show clearly that the most effective early years settings had alert practitioners who were ready to be part of children's freely chosen play and conversation, but without taking over that experience for their own adult purposes. Genuinely helpful adults offered comments – not a stream of directive questions – and they joined in the play on children's terms. The research has also tracked the significant impact of a positive home learning environment.

Best practice is that there is a relaxed flow between experiences that are initiated by children, those initiated by adults and who leads at any given time. Adults are partners in the play and conversation. A visitor, like myself, needs to talk with practitioners to understand the meaning of what has happened. I often need to hear the back story to what I can observe on a single visit.

Look closer: The moving walkway

During the morning of my visit to Ladybirds Pre-School, I watched as three boys worked their way across a significant stretch of the outdoor area towards the door to the inside of Ladybirds. They had a system of four milk crates, which formed the basic walkway. But they moved forward by the boy at the end lifting up a crate, passing it along to the front boy who put in down in front to form the next section. Sometimes they had two crates moving from back to front at the same time.

The boys focused on their system, taking care with placement. They had an efficient and relatively speedy

---

Links to your practice

You aim for a positive continuity between children's home life and their time with you. Partnership with parents starts from first contact and what you understand from those early conversations helps you to respect and reflect a child's existing interests when they join you. There is no sense in trying to make the two sources of experience identical. However, there is every need to make connections for and with children between the different parts of their life.

- In Ladybirds Pre-School, one child was intrigued by knights and castles. He brought in his favourite book about the subject which led to some enthusiastic building in the setting. A parent whose child also attends the setting is involved in reenactments of historical events and has agreed to visit within the summer term with his outfit and weapons.

- In Skerne Park reception class each child has their own 'My Geneva Woods Book', which documents their personal experience of their weekly trip into the woodland. Children add their drawings, emergent writing or explain to an adult to scribe what they want written verbatim. The books and the substantial wall display in the classroom also include what some children do on outdoor trips with their own family. One example was a description of what two boys had enjoyed in the same woodland area on trips with their Boys' Brigade – an experience they also raised in spontaneous conversation during the woodland outing that I joined. The shared display and each child's own book also included recent photos from when most parents had joined a special family trip with the class.

In what ways have you created these direct links between family life and children's experience during their time with you?

approach. One boy announced what was clearly the aim of the whole team: "We're going to get all the way to the door, OK!". When the walkway team had almost made it to their goal, another child called out: "And I'm going to give you a medal". As the boys triumphantly stepped off at the door, an adult close by said: "Well done! You did it!".

I was told the back story to this child-initiated event. Earlier in the week, a practitioner had noticed the enthusiasm with which children were building with the generous store of milk crates available in the Ladybirds outdoor space. She suggested: "Would you like to try a new game?" Her idea was to create a moving walkway with the technique that the boys chose to use again on the day of my visit. On the first occasion children had constructed a substantial walkway all across the garden. The practitioner had introduced the idea then of awarding a medal. On the day of my visit, the practitioner had already printed a sequence of photos from the earlier enterprise, creating a long visual story of the milk crate walkway. The run of photos was laminated and she fixed it to the door of the shed. Children looked at the photos and commented throughout the day.

Milk crates for clambering and jumping off

A significant group of children from the morning and afternoon group in Ladybirds were involved in an absorbing physical play sequence that depended on a built structure of milk crates and wooden planks. A practitioner was close by throughout this play – the same adult for sustained runs of time. She was directly responsive to what the children wanted to do, as well as discretely checking if the current structure had shifted and needed to be realigned.

In the morning there was a great deal of jumping from a structure that was four crates high. Children requested and were given a handhold to make the jump. The structure was close to a strong, soft rope that had been securely fixed across a section of the garden. After training in the importance of physically active play from Jabadao (www.jabadao.org), the Ladybirds team had sought a way that children could explore hanging suspended by the grip of their own hands.

Led initially by two girls, the climb-and-jump use of the milk crate tower turned into a stretch-and-hang by both hands. An adult remained by the structure and provided the level of help requested by each individual child. A series of girls and boys were keen to climb up and hang by their hands over and over again. Some

needed adult help to reach for the rope, some wanted to be held lightly as they hung and some liked to be eased down by an adult arm around their waist, when they were ready to drop to the ground. However, as children practised this skill out of choice, I observed how individuals became more adept over the session. Some children, girls and boys, reached the point of confidence where they stretched out, seized the rope, let it take their weight and then dropped – all with no required assistance from the adult.

The milk crate structure continued to be extended by the children. The afternoon group built further on what had been left from the morning. It became a longer structure with lower sections which enabled a queue to form – and children chatted as they moved patiently towards their turn. Access to the structure also then included two wooden planks. By the end of the afternoon two children were attempting, within their individual turn, to move along the rope, moving their hands. At one point a girl suggested and fetched a large flat cushion to provide a slightly softer landing point.

The uncertainty in the EYFS over the balance of child-initiated versus adult-led activities has left some practitioners anxious to find a reliable numerical proportion for planned activities by the adults. Some discussion strands on early years Internet forums highlight a misunderstanding that all adult-led times are focused group sessions – this is not true, see page 4. Some of the concerns expressed in the early years forums revolve around how many group times you should have within a day. This query is actually the wrong question – as some of the posted replies sensibly explain. The more important question is around what leads you to believe that bringing young children together in a focused group time is the best approach. What are you hoping to offer to them, in what ways are your plans directly linked with children's current interests and understanding and – just as important –- what makes you think an adult-led group is the best way to support this focus of learning?

Look closer: Group time that belongs to the children

In Garfield reception class, the two teachers come together with their groups at the beginning and end of each morning and afternoon. For the rest of the day, the children experience free flow between the well-resourced indoor and outdoor environment shared by the two classes and the team of four practitioners. The focus of these group times is that children reflect on what has happened, discuss evolving plans and share their current projects. The adult facilitates the conversational exchanges and individual contributions. But the reception team are consistent that their role is not to teach children along pre-planned and firmly adult-led lines.

■ Several children discussed their morning activity (see page 34 about the soldiers' camp). Marie, a focus child for this week (see page 24), discussed her plans for a puppet theatre. She showed her frame and described her frustration that it kept breaking. The teacher added that she had asked someone else for advice and the suggestion was that they need to focus on making 'strong corners' for the frame. Other children joined actively in the discussion about how to solve this practical problem. Another child had done a drawing of the theatre, which the adult referred to as 'your design'. The children talked around the project some more and then Marie used puppets, and three chosen child companions to tell her created story.

■ By the end of the day come together time Marie had finalised her narrative – a version of the Sleeping Beauty story. She told her story with a puppet and a theatre created out of an open cardboard box. She was followed by another girl who told yet another

version of Sleeping Beauty through four characters represented by paper shapes fixed to lolly sticks.

Please consider all the different aspects of learning that are reflected in this example. Think about the events recalled and planned and the children's ability to participate in and enjoy this kind of discussion.

What is meant by individualised learning?

The revised EYFS statutory framework (DfE, 2012) is much reduced from the first version. Some of the explanatory paragraphs from the 2008 EYFS are necessary to make sense of the personal approach to children's learning.

The EYFS sets standards to enable early years providers to reflect the rich and personalised experience that many parents give their children at home. Like parents, providers should deliver individualised learning, development and care that enhances the development of the children in their care and gives those children the best possible start in life. (DCSF, 2008, paragraph 1.13, page 9).

This quotation makes a powerful statement about the nature of children's experiences up to the end of reception class: the final year of children's early years stage in England. The clear message was that best early years practice is a personalised, home-like experience, wherever it takes place. The model is that of a happy home and not that of a school classroom – even one with the excellent practice I have observed in some primary schools from Year 1 onwards.

Guidance published after the main 2008 EYFS materials progressively replaced the phrase 'learning and teaching' with 'learning, playing and interacting' (National Strategies, 2009, 2010). This shift seemed to be a belated recognition that, for a proportion of the early years workforce, 'teaching' meant adult-directed activities and a primary school image of how to run a day. In a Birth to Five framework serious thought about choice of words was even more important.

The focus of the 2012 EYFS on 'school readiness' raises concerns, since only a developmentally appropriate interpretation of this transition will benefit young children. It is useful to revisit this statement from the 2008 Statutory Framework.

> It is crucial to their future success that children's earliest experiences help to build a secure foundation for learning throughout their school years and beyond. Practitioners must be sensitive to the individual development of each child to ensure that the activities they undertake are suitable for the stage they have reached. Children need to be stretched, but not pushed beyond their capabilities, so they can continue to enjoy learning (2008, paragraph 1.18, page 10).

Along with the previous mention of the home-like model, this quotation was a clear message that the role of early years practitioners is to help young children to stretch from their current skills and understanding – not to give them one almighty shove.

These key quotations enabled practitioners and managers to make sense of the overall requirements about best practice on planning and organisation. In the 2008 EYFS, best practice focused on ensuring that every child received an enjoyable and challenging experience, tailored to their individual needs. The revised EYFS states in the introduction that this framework seeks to provide a secure foundation through opportunities 'which are planned around the needs and interests of each individual child and are assessed and reviewed regularly' (DfE, 2012, page 2).

Individual or personalised learning is definitely not about detailed, written plans of everything that will be made available for each child and in what way. Respect for children as individuals sits comfortably with a flexible approach to forward planning and plenty of adult attention for creating an interesting and easily accessible learning environment from which children can choose and organise themselves. Early years practitioners cannot possibly take an individual approach, if they have embraced a one-size-fits-all in terms of planned activities.

In Randolph Beresford Early Years Centre the team has discussed at length the issues around creating an environment in which adults are play partners with babies, toddlers and children. They have reflected as a team on how to put their energy into sustained involvement with children's chosen play and away from trying to organise the play in advance. Their approach focuses on how to provide continuity of learning, to view a situation and experiences through children's eyes. The team describe the approach as 'picking up the threads running through children's learning' and they adjust this perspective, as appropriate for the full age range from babies to four-year-olds who attend the centre.

During my visit I saw many instances of how practitioners brought individualised learning alive. Here are just two examples.

Look closer: Going with the flow of children's immediate interests

Best practice across the age range of early childhood is to notice and respond to young children's current interests and the focus of their chosen efforts. Practitioners need to be especially sensitive and in-the-moment with babies, toddlers and very young children. In the outdoor area of the under-threes in the Randolph Beresford Centre I observed practitioners who remained alert to what had caught the attention of toddlers and twos.

The adults' comments related directly to what a child had chosen to do, such as struggling to put on clothing and a large sombrero hat from the dressing up store. One adult got on a bike to join two children on their own bikes and one pushing a doll in a buggy. They drove in repeated circuits and variations around the garden, with the adult checking, "Which way do you want to go?" and "What would you like to do now?" Physically active play came to a temporary halt as practitioners joined in what had suddenly caught children's attention, like looking over the low fence to watch the older children in the other part of the garden or listening to the sounds of birds.

Several children were keen to clamber along and through the long, raised obstacle course, sometimes carrying a doll at the same time. An adult remained by the equipment, commenting: "Are you going to have a try?", "That's it! Pull yourself up", "Half way now", "Are you climbing over now?" and "Are you ready for dolly to come down?" Help was given if these young children indicated they wanted a hand.

The practitioners had created a raised platform in the garden by a layout of hollow, wooden blocks. A series of young children were keen to manoeuvre their doll and buggy up and over this platform. This rather challenging physical task for very young children was, I was told, a chosen focus on many days. The practitioners responded to this activity with the same seriousness that the children and toddlers showed – it mattered to them and was worth their time and energy. At different times over the first part of the morning, adults commented on children's efforts: "Up you go", "On and off" and "Oh, your baby fell off". Help was offered with: "Can you get the buggy down that way?", "Can you work out how to do it? You did it a minute ago" and "Would you like some help?" Individual young children repeated several cycles of up, on, off and round. Children usually managed the turn taking, sometimes using words like 'my turn', 'your turn' and 'ready'.

. . . .

Making bubbles and where it led

In one of the centre rooms for three- and four-year-olds, a wide range of mark making resources were available on a table, other resources as well as a sink were close by. Several children were busy with creations of their own choosing. The practitioner remained close and was highly responsive to what the children wanted to do with the materials. She had set up the table with extra supplies of feathers today, but there was no expectation that children should be making feather paintings in preference to anything else.

One child, Katie, was undecided as to how to use the resources and the adult helped by talking her through her decision, "You need to decide between your two plans. Which one would you like to do first?". Katie decided to make a bubble mixture, which could be blown. The adult supported this plan and reminded Katie about the basic technique. Otherwise the adult asked guiding questions when Katie got stuck and the child replied, decided and experimented until she had a workable mixture. The adult commented in ways like: "What do you think is the problem?", "Is it (the mixture) too thick or too thin?", "Shall we try a little more water?", "It's not working, is it? What could we try now?" and "Look what you've done. It's working now."

Over time Katie, and up to five other children, were very active in blowing paint bubbles – sometimes a whole cluster like a bunch of grapes. They blew onto paper and watched the different effects. Since they had mixed black paint, the children also became intrigued by the dramatic effect of getting the paint on their hands. The same adult was relaxed about the paint, helping children wipe themselves only when they wished. The practitioner suggested using the mirror to view their "beautiful black gloves" and how the paint looked, "like black lipstick" and "having a nice beard". The children were very enthusiastic about the effects they had created and there was a general agreement, "to do it again tomorrow".

Over this time, the practitioner responded in a relaxed way to several other children who came up for a chat or for company. A child wanted to make the adult some glasses, another child said she felt tired and the adult talked about possible ways to have a restful time. The practitioner shared her attention between the children in an even-handed way, keeping track of the different enterprises going on within this space.

Meaningful experiences

Some early years provision has long established practice focusing on individual children, their current development and their personal interests. Those practitioners who are experienced in a flexible approach continue to discuss the issues and consider the balance of what they offer. However, the EYFS emphasis on child-initiated activities and learning has posed a challenge to the less flexible approaches to organising children's day and a view of planning that places adults as the deciders and leaders most of the time.

Young children need a personal experience, not days in which they are treated as one of many little bodies in a group. They learn through meaningful experiences, not a list of pre-planned activities that supposedly support a single aspect of development or required learning outcome. The adult outlook on time and timing is also part of an individual approach. It is not always clear immediately what any child has learned from an experience like a conversation, or an activity which has genuinely engaged their interest. There is often a time lag – later that same day, later this week or sometimes even weeks later.

Putting children's interests at the heart of your practice is not about stepping away from an adult role for organisation. It is about taking on a different kind of organising role as a helpful practitioner. Giving full rein to young children's interests does not mean chaos and it does not mean a total lack of responsible boundaries. Plenty of child-initiated experiences usually mean playful and highly productive movement by children of useful resources around your learning environment. There may be 'mess', but it is very purposeful mess and children should be involved in joint tidying up at the end of a session or day.

The quality of experiences for young children stands or falls on what you do: how you interact with children on a personal level and within an ongoing relationship with them and their families. Observation, planning and a developmentally appropriate approach to assessment are all significant contributions to best early years practice. However, paperwork and background organisation – even the most sensible forms of documentation – do not in themselves make a positive difference to the quality of children's early experiences. Only real people can do that: familiar practitioners who are in an ongoing relationship with children – adults who listen, look, think, talk and join in play and conversation.

Being a partner in play

Early years practitioners need to be comfortable in the role of a play companion, who will be welcome to young children – rather than someone to be avoided as a nuisance and a play spoiler. Adults can make a positive difference to early learning but the route is as an equal play partner, sometimes called a 'co-player'.

The EYFS materials have made a consistent stand in support of play-based experiences for young children and for early years practitioners to focus on learning through play. The approach is confirmed in the revised Statutory Framework with: "*Each area of learning and development must be implemented through planned, purposeful play and through a mix of adult-led and child-initiated activity*" (DfE, 2012: paragraph 1.9, page 6). That middle phrase – planned, purposeful play continued to be symbolic of problems that have arisen from a particular outlook on what is meant in practice by learning through play. The Welsh Foundation Phase has similar issues within the guidance (2008) with phrases like 'well-planned play', 'structured educational play' and 'active educational play'. Please think about the nature of real play for children – experiences that are full of playfulness and to which children themselves feel highly committed.

Play belongs to children; adults are visitors in that world of exploration.

- Early years practitioners are welcome guests when they show respect and genuine enthusiasm to be a partner in playful enterprises.

Food for thought

A well-informed adult play partner also understands the ways in which playful enterprises evolve over the years of early childhood. Some resource materials about the stages of social play still claim that babies and children under two years of age play alone and that there is little interaction with other children. It is also sometimes claimed that two-year-olds watch and play alongside but do not ever play together.

This misinformation does not survive ten minutes of unbiased observation of babies, toddlers and very young children. Their play patterns are different from those of over-threes. But the younger children do make direct contact with each other. When circumstances enable very young children to become familiar with peers, or children of a different age, they can be observed in joint explorations and shared games to which they return day after day.

- How can play still be playful if adults determine many of the choices available to children in their play?

- Adults disrespect the spontaneity of playing children when they seize control of the play through directive suggestions and questioning.

- 'Play with a purpose' is no longer play if adults' intentions are what matter most and they are the arbiters of what is worthwhile, relevant or productive.

- Genuine play is seasoned with uncertainty. Who knows what will happen?

- Children often pause to resolve an uncertainty that arises within their pretend play or shared construction project. Uncertainty provokes discussion and exploration.

- However, uncertainty can be very unsettling for practitioners who have been taught it is legitimate to pre-package activities to deliver specific outcomes and still call it 'play'.

- Adults, who trust the power of play, put their thoughtfulness into a learning environment that invites choice. They create time, and organise routines, that enable play experiences to evolve and flow.

- In a playful environment there is a sense of shared control between children and adults, who can and should still be the responsible grown-up.

Some significant experiences, which children regard as well worth their time and effort, are not play as the word is meant by many adults.

- Children are keen to be active participants in the ordinary domestic routines. Their involvement provides significant scope for them to learn.

- Increased knowledge and understanding is often woven back into children's self-chosen play, including their imaginative sequences.

- Children do not only learn through play. We have to ask 'what for?' if children are given a play version instead of direct involvement in experiences like shopping, gardening or cooking.

We want a virtuous circle in which play is largely determined by children and not by what adults fully prepared earlier. Engaged adults can then look out for what has truly seized children's energy and interest. You tuck in behind children's enthusiasm. A welcome play partner adds something of direct relevance: a comment, an idea that connects closely, further resources or a helping hand that is needed in this enterprise. Your adult thinking power is focussed on planning for the possibilities of play rather than attempting to micro-manage the details of play itself.

Adults as play partners show respect for what interests children. Babies and toddlers definitely have keen current interests. But these can seem less obvious to practitioners, if they are looking for the kind of play more typical of over threes. Certainly you do not depend entirely on what any child can say in words. You have to use your eyes as well as your ears to notice and respond to individual interests and the intriguing angles that children bring to an experience – whether their own direct choice, or an activity or event introduced by the practitioner.

Close observation often shows that older babies, toddlers and young children repeat the same actions in order to find out whether the consequence is the same. This basic fact about how the world works may seem obvious to adults; but it is far from obvious to young children. As a baby, how do you know that a toy dropped from a certain height will make a satisfying bang every time it hits the floor? You do not know for sure until you, the baby or toddler, have conducted this personal experiment several times – and maybe again tomorrow and then again because it is just such fun. Practitioners need sound child development knowledge to be reassured that this kind of chosen 'doing it again and again' is a normal, welcome state of play for young children. The behaviour is not a sign of possible autistic spectrum disorder.

Respect for schemas

One way of tuning-in to the current interest of young children is to observe their patterns in play in what they choose to do with their current skills and available resources. Schemas are an observable pattern that forms the basis of deliberate exploration for an individual child for some time. You would not use the word to describe brief actions that do not recur. Young children can be persistent in following their preferred way of exploring, but they will apply their schema to a range of resources.

The playful behaviour of very young babies is closely linked to their increasing control over their own bodies, including hands and fingers and the coordination of holding and grasping with what they see. As older babies gain greater control over their body they are able to make deliberate movements, connecting with objects or familiar adults or children. As older babies turn into physically mobile toddlers, their exploratory schemas of shaking or throwing develop into sequences of how they act upon their world. The approach of schemas or play patterns has been useful when practitioners, or parents, are tempted to view purposeful young play as just a mess. An additional adult problem is sometimes that young children are judged to be involved in repetitive, pointless play and need to be enticed into doing something different. Being 'schema wise', as Lisa Gadsby describes it, can be a positive route away from disrespect for a child's chosen interest and links closely with planning led through resources within the learning environment, rather than separate adult-led activities.

Respect for schemas is still compatible with being a responsible grown up.

- Some children show a long-term interest in moving items or other children around the environment, bagging up and reorganising elsewhere – a transporting schema. It is reasonable to guide children towards their responsibility to bring back transported resources to their storage area when they have finished or at full tidy-up time at the end of the day or session. It is unreasonable to tell children they cannot move items away from a given area.

- Perhaps one or more children are fascinated by joining things together or taking them apart – a schema of connection and disconnection. It is fair enough to say that the current enterprise of tying string between many items and pieces of equipment needs to be undertaken in a way that does not create tripwires. It would be poor practice to stop the busy creators of a viaduct on the grounds that they cannot spend all day with guttering and milk crates.

The emotional environment

The revised supporting guidance to the EYFS (Early Education, 2012) continues to emphasise the importance of enabling environments. Babies and children can only exercise a choice from what they can see, or know is available, in your home as a childminder or in their group setting. So their ability to initiate, and steadily organise themselves as independent learners, is shaped by their physical environment. However, children's options are not only influenced by what they can get their hands on. The quality of their experiences is also shaped by the reaction of familiar adults who create the atmosphere of any early years provision.

Links to your practice

The role of being a play partner can help reflection and discussion about how best to behave as a supportive adult with young children.

- Free flow play, and respect for child-initiated learning, does not mean letting young children run riot with no boundaries at all.

- Nor does it mean dividing up the day or session into 'free play' when adults largely keep their distance, busy with other tasks, and 'structured or focused activity time', when adults dominate what happens and how.

- The problem with this unwise division is that children would often like more adult input in the 'free play' times and less adult dominance in the 'structured' times.

Within a team or the support of a childminding network, you need to work through concerns and uncertainties. These are understandable, given some of the unwise advice directed at early years practitioners in recent times.

Do some people worry about when and how to contribute to children's play? Support can be needed to avoid either extreme.

- Practitioners may be anxious about 'interfering', when children definitely need direct help or the intervention of the adult as diplomat. This reticence sometimes means that the adult then has to intervene at a more directive level, because play has in one way or another got out of hand.

- Alternatively, some adults may be too swift to offer a suggestion, when children could be helped to work their way towards ideas. They feel they are doing 'nothing' as a more equal play partner, or fear that another adult will accuse them of 'just' sitting about.

More experienced and confident practitioners can sometimes support by being present with a colleague. Your aim is to support the confidence of a less experienced team member, but also to show good practice by your own actions. When you are part of the play, you can model being a supportive play partner by direct example. Sometimes you will be watching alongside a colleague. It can help to discretely voice out loud what you are thinking to this fellow adult. You might quietly say for example: "I think that Liam and George are steering their bikes carefully. I'm keeping an eye, but I don't think we need to stop them." After an action you might share: "I thought it was important that I offered my help to Kayleigh. But I would have taken 'no' for an answer".

Me in!

So, the revised EYFS continues to highlight not only the indoor and outdoor physical environment, but also the emotional environment. As a visitor to any provision, it is possible to feel this atmosphere relatively quickly and to recognise how observable behaviour of practitioners contributes to this sense, as much as – probably even more than – the physical characteristics of the learning environment. Child-initiated learning, resting on appropriate resources and time and space for child choice, is dependent on the behaviour and outlook of the adults.

Appropriately relaxed early years practitioners are physically close to young children and show their genuine interest in what this baby, toddler or child is keen to do at the moment. Children can follow the buzz of their own learning, when familiar adults are comfortable about sharing control and decision making with children over what will happen today. The emotional environment is very different, if practitioners' comfort zones are defined by a fixed plan for what play resources are laid out today and how any activity will evolve.

Look closer: Playing with the sand

In Start Point Sholing Early Years Centre practitioners remain easily available to the children. Considerable adult thought has gone into the indoor and outdoor learning environment, so that children can have significant scope for making their own choices as they play and talk.

On the day of my visit, twos and young threes were busy around a sand tray equipped with a wide range of containers, plastic bottles, funnels and scoops. Children spent considerable time working with sand during the morning and in the afternoon. There was a great deal of filling and pouring. For much of the time an adult was sitting at the same level as the children. She showed interest in what they wanted to do and sometimes commented. For instance, she said that a bottle was "full", when a young girl was trying to get more sand into the bottle via the funnel. The child had looked puzzled that no more sand was running through the funnel.

One girl had filled a container with sand and indicated that she wanted to "cook it". The practitioner checked: "Do you want to put it in the oven?" and when the answer was a clear nod, the adult pulled the toy cooker closer to the area with the sand. This may seem like a minor action on the part of the adult, but it made a big difference to the children. The first child, and then accompanied by a second girl, became very engaged in filling up containers with sand, cooking their 'cakes' in the toy oven and bringing them out, after a short while. They also started to 'cook' bowls of dry pasta, which was available in a low tuff spot close by. Moving the cooker enabled them to extend their play without constantly walking around their peers, to the cooker and back again.

In the afternoon, sand was still available but this time in a low, shallow container. Children were still using scoops

Links to your practice

The point about schemas is that they should help you to notice and respond to sustained play patterns. It is not wise to link planning exclusively to schemas. I have encountered practitioners who feel they cannot plan from a child's interests, because they have been unable to identify a schema from their list. Valuable play does not have to fit a schema, nor do you have to create another schema on a lengthening list.

A keen den builder is not necessarily operating within a schema of enveloping. Sometimes he and his fellow builders are just building a den and that should be quite enough for the practitioner who notices this busy activity. You consider what you could offer for children's interest in terms of how do we build a bigger, better and more stable den. Even if the lead builder does have a track record of enveloping, practitioners should not lose sense of the current content within the longer term category. The focus for now is the den and the fact that today the children have decided that it is the home of a league of superhero tigers. Your attention should be on the moment, going with the children's imaginative flow and not on planning how one child might extend his schema of enveloping.

and bottles. Then one young girl took off her shoes plus socks and experimented with walking in the sand, looking at the impact of her bare feet. Another child watched and then took off her tights to walk in the sand. The first girl had gone to get herself a rolling pin and returned to roll the sand, looking closely again at the effect on soft sand. Over the afternoon, as well as the morning, the sand and pasta spread over this part of the indoor environment. Practitioners swept up just enough to prevent skidding.

. . . .

Sharing a book with a baby and young child

An area called the Safe Haven provides a comfortable space surrounded by low level wooden room dividers. A practitioner sat with a baby in her lap. She followed the baby's immediate interests: looking in the direction that the baby gazed and commenting on what had apparently caught the baby's attention. She smiled back at the baby and joined in raspberry blowing. A three-year-old boy came and went several times into the Safe Haven. He wanted to show the baby different items and he opened and shut the gate each time without assistance. Then the boy came with a book that he wanted to share with the practitioner. She made space for him and asked him to turn the pages, since she was holding the baby safe on her lap. The boy snuggled up, and in an emotionally warm home-like exchange, he enjoyed the book and the baby gazed too.

Adult respect for child-initiated learning means time and space for active learning: that situation in which children are busy participants in their own next steps and possible lines of enquiry. Active learning is not necessarily physically lively; children may be intellectually and emotionally very active whilst choosing to remain physically in the same place. However, purposeful physical activity is an important element of following children's interests. Purposeful means in terms of children's own wish to enjoy energetic movement. It will be their choice today to practise specific emerging skills and challenge themselves physically.

Enjoyable challenge, and learning, is also emotional – "I really want to do this, although it is a bit scary" – and intellectual – "I am going to work out (or remember) how to do this". Children need a sense of emotional security in order to develop as young learners: that it is alright to be uncertain, puzzled or to make mistakes, because that is genuinely how you extend your learning when adults are on your side.

Look closer: An outdoors experience

The significance of the emotional environment 'travels' with a group of familiar young children and adults wherever they go. Shared experiences are part of the continuing relationship between practitioners and the individual children with whom they spend so many hours.

A group of 16 three- and four-year-olds from Stocksfield Avenue Nursery Class go once a week with their practitioners to visit an area of woodland just outside

Newcastle upon Tyne. The outdoor visits are part of a joint project with Sightlines Initiative (www.sightlines-initiative.com). The group take their time over the morning visit and relish the walk down to the woodland as well as the return trip back uphill, to where the coach is parked. Children choose to stop and stare, to look closely at flowers and black slugs and to listen as the sounds of the stream become clearer as the group descended into the valley. The aim is that children gain direct first-hand experience of the natural environment.

Over the term the group had steadily progressed further into the wooded area with each trip. On the morning I joined the trip they followed the path all the way down to reach the stream. Some parts were more of a scramble for young children but they looked for ways to clamber. They also watched children and adults who were part way down the track and chose their strategy, sometimes that of moving down on their bottom, with or without handholds. Adults encouraged and offered direct help if a child was clearly uneasy without a hand.

One small group of children was heard to say that the most challenging section was, "the scariest place in the world". This pronouncement was tinged with excitement rather than fear and there was a real sense of achievement on children's faces when they reached the flat area around the stream, and also on their return climb. Once on the flatter sections around the stream, children had time to get a sense of their surroundings, this newly encountered space within the woodland. They chose to stand and look, some individuals longer than others, before they start "adventuring", as the Sightlines team describe it.

. . . .

Children confident within their environment

In Kennet Day Nursery, mobile under-threes can move between the two spaces: Minnows which is the dedicated space for babies and young toddlers and Dragonflies, the home base of older toddlers and twos. The two spaces are divided by a low wooden room divider, with a gate. I watched as a series of these slightly older children were able to open the gate to enter and leave Minnows. They all took the trouble to shut the gate as well. Two children had asked for soft toys from the cupboard. The practitioner opened the door, so they could see and each child pointed and then took their choice back into the Dragonflies space. Another child came and selected other resources to take back to the other side.

I watched as Harry and another two-year-old moved independently from Dragonflies into Minnows and settled down out of their own choice to explore a low basket of cylinder and ball shapes which have magnetic end pieces. The two children explored the pieces and joined them together. They then started to see what else could hold the pieces and tried a metal door hinge.

The practitioner was sitting on the floor and responded to their interest by pointing out a low metal frame, used for hanging toys at a suitable height for a baby lying on her back. (The only baby in the room at the time was sleeping in the cot.) The practitioner wondered aloud "they will stick to the metal".

The two children held the pieces to the frame and found that they could attach some shapes so they hung, but others moved slowly down the side struts. The practitioner commented on what was happening: "I wonder how that happens", adding after a pause: "It's because they have things called magnets". She commented on the different ways that the shapes reacted with, "it spun around, didn't it", "they're sliding down" and "they're stuck on there". The two children picked up on the words for 'slide' and 'stuck'.

The Kennet team show a sustained interest in what engages individual babies, toddlers and children, or small, busy groups. Practitioners sit at the level of children or swiftly get down to children's eye level. There is a strong message to children that this adult is not about to move away.

> Communicative adults:
> communicative children

Ongoing concern about the limited communication skills of some young children led to a national initiative for England – Every Child a Talker. Some children do not experience the kind of simple early exchanges that build the skills of listening and talking. Their developmental delay cannot be explained by a disability that affects learning language; the problem is that of restricted communication from adult users of their language(s). The programme could equally well be called Every Adult a Listener.

Simple, personal and spontaneous works best of all. Genuine conversation – with anyone – is a shared enterprise in which both partners have an approximately equal share in talking time. Young children learn about the give-and-take of a real and enjoyable conversation by experiences with communicative adults. Even young babies start this learning journey, because familiar adults respond to a baby's looks, gestures and meaningful sound making.

Look closer: Conversation while building
In Randolph Beresford Early Years Centre one practitioner was sitting in the block corner, a quiet space to the side of one room and, over a period of time, was busy building and talking as a responsive play partner with one and then two children (three and four-years-old). For much of the time the children's fascination was with constructing tall, single block towers and watching them fall, or giving them a nudge to make them tumble dramatically.

It fell down like THAT!

The adult eased the turn taking, when that was necessary, as well as reminding the children that it was not OK to knock down someone else's tower, unless they invited you to do that. She commented in a directly relevant way about the height of the towers and used her hand to indicate how tall. She did not try to count the bricks, since number of bricks was not the chosen focus of these children. They showed interest in the relative height of each tower, as well as building taller and taller. The adult enjoyed the tension with the children of "It's wobbling! Is it going to go?" and then "it came tumbling down". One child talked about their enterprise with "put it higher and higher and higher" and explained to another child who had just joined them: "It fell down like that". Another child shared: "Do you know what happened to my one? It fell down. We made it higher".

During the long building and tumbling down sequence the adult remained sitting and attentive. There were sustained periods when she looked and listened, but did not try to fill a companionable silence for no good reason. She also responded immediately to a range of conversations initiated by one or both children, which had nothing to do with the building project. These subjects included the delights of cake, and chocolate cake in particular, the exploits of the fictional character Ben 10©, the shoes children were wearing today and how one of the blocks became, for a short time, a pretend parcel.

. . . .

The experiment to make dirty water clean

Garfield reception class plans through special attention each week to the chosen projects of three focus children. During the day of my visit, four-year-old Jaleel was one of the focus children and he was keen to research about water and how to make dirty water clean again. Following a conversation with Jaleel yesterday, the practitioner had borrowed a book about doing experiments from the science specialist teacher in the primary school.

This focused enterprise lasted for well over an hour in the morning. For this period Jaleel, and his chosen companions, had the full attention of the reception teacher. He remained with Jaleel but continued to be responsive to other children who came up to comment on the experiment or to bring him up to date with other events, such as the story they were writing.

The adult guided Jaleel and the other children through the steps of several related experiments, helping them to check back in the science book. He used open-ended questions to support them such as "where are we going to find soil?" (they needed earth to make the dirty water), "what do you think will happen when we pour the water through?" and "why do you think it's not clean yet?". The series of related experiments did not all go smoothly, but the adult eased the difficulties with the approach of, "what's the problem?" and "what can we do about it?". Jaleel and his fellow experimenters went off to find resources they needed in other parts of the reception area – indoors and outside – and returned.

For about half of this time Jaleel had a small group of children working with him on the experiment. After some sustained experimenting, his companions decided to leave and do something else – which was fine – and Jaleel continued with the support of the practitioner. They got stuck at one point and together wondered about different possible methods for filtering the dirty water and what a particular instruction in the book might mean. Jaleel was active in this speculation, saying firmly at one point: "I think that's what it means" and later: "I think I'm doing it right and you did it wrong".

At one point they decided to get some more equipment from the science specialist teacher in the primary school section of Garfield and then found that some different paper for the filtering process did seem to work better. In the end they had identified a way to make dirty

water noticeably cleaner through a process of filtration. Throughout this whole process the adult listened at least as much as he talked and left pauses for Jaleel to think, as well as initiate his own ideas.

Children benefit from enjoyable exchanges with practitioners who are genuinely interested to make discoveries through the medium of conversation. Questions are a valuable use of language but can be mis-used or over-used. The most useful questions that adults pose to children are those that open up possibilities. Practitioners are sometimes tempted to ask closed, checking questions like "what colour is this?" or "how many are there?". If young children understand any given abstract concept, they will show you through their play and conversation. If they have not yet unravelled this way of describing the world, then your question will puzzle them. In my observations, I have noticed that even when young children cooperate by answering this kind of closed question, they are considerably less animated than when they reply to the more interesting adult enquiries that start with, "I wonder…"or "How does that...?".

Look closer: A lesson from children about questions worth asking

Over lunchtime in Kennet Day Nursery I was part of a conversation, with appropriate question-and-answer led by Melanie, two-and-a-half, and Tamara, nearly three years of age. I had bought a sandwich for my lunch and sat next to Melanie, who was finishing her lunch. She started by asking: "Why are you eating that?". I explained that there had not been any spare lunch, so I had gone out to buy myself the sandwich. Melanie listened and then asked another: "why are you doing that?". I gave a further explanation that my tummy had started to rumble, so I knew I was hungry. As a visitor, I did not understand until later, in conversation with the manager, that Melanie – and Tamara who had joined us – were probably asking a slightly different question. When staff need to buy themselves some lunch, they eat in the staff room. So the question was more likely to have been why I was eating something that was not what they viewed as the proper lunch.

Tamara started another topic of conversation by saying: "My Mummy will pick me up later" and asked me: "Will your Mummy pick you up?". I explained that since I was a grown up, I could go home by myself. Tamara thought for a moment and then asked, "Did your Mummy pick you up when you was little?". I said yes and agreed that, when you are young you cannot go home on your own. Tamara then chose to tell me about her family: that she had a Mummy and a Daddy and a brother. Then she asked me a series of questions – put courteously and with space for me to reply. Tamara was interested to know who was in my family, did I still live with my Mummy and Daddy and did my children (I had explained I had two) still live in my home?

I was struck by this exchange, led by two young children, neither of them past their third birthday. They were confident that a visitor to their nursery would be happy to chat with them. They understood the nature of a genuine conversation and they showed the key social skills:

- They asked questions to which they did not currently know the answer and would like to find out that answer now.

- They paused, listened and looked attentively while I answered their questions.

- Tamara shared something personal about her own life and linked her questions to that subject as she inquired about my family life.

- Their questions and comments were connected in a conversational flow that made sense.

What is 'sustained shared thinking'?

The EPPE research described the positive ways that some early years practitioners come alongside children in their chosen enterprises and adjust their own, adult contribution to support and extend children's learning. The EPPE team called this pattern of communicative interaction 'sustained shared thinking'. You can find transcripts of some exchanges in the report by Iram Siraj-Blatchford et al. (2002).

The EYFS (2008) promoted the importance of sustained shared thinking. However, the guidance does not provide much descriptive information about what the phrase means, to support practitioners who are unfamiliar with the EPPE research reports. Also, this practical concept makes little sense without the secure foundation of understanding the essentials of communicating with babies and young children described on page 19. Without this essential grasp, less sure practitioners can think they are undertaking sustained shared thinking when, in fact, they are directing an exchange through closed questions and leaving little or no conversational space for children. It is useful to consider sustained shared thinking (SST) through one element at a time.

Sustained: In sustained shared thinking the exchange between adult and child, or a very small number of children, lasts more than a moment. SST is not about adults 'popping in', dropping off a comment or question and zooming off again. Adults stay for a reasonable length of time – sitting with children or otherwise close to them and fully engaged in the focus of attention. The examples from the EPPE research also show that communicative sequences which engage children do not necessarily happen within a single conversation. When adult and children are in a sustained relationship, then either partner often returns to a conversational focus after time and some thinking.

It is always useful to remind ourselves of important basics. Some readers will also be responsible for guiding less experienced colleagues who are uncertain.

- Communicative adults listen and look with children at least as much as talk. You need to get and stay on a child's level and make friendly eye contact.

- Avoid rushing to fill the gap of silence. Consider it as possible thinking time and trust the power of the pause.

- Communicative adults do not always have to be saying something out loud. You communicate positive messages to babies and children when you also gaze at what has caught their attention and look interested.

- A considerable amount of attentive communication from adults to very young children is about awareness of gesture and all the non-verbal clues. This attentiveness to body language should continue when the recognisable words start to appear.

- Make sure you have a child's attention before you start to talk – also be patient when they are busy with something or someone else. If in doubt, use touch, eye contact and a smile or their name.

- Once you are in conversation with a child, what you say needs to connect with what you are both doing. You might

be playing together or walking around the garden. It makes sense to point out something of interest and definitely to respond to whatever has caught the child's attention.

- The best exchanges are relatively simple sequences of turn taking over talking and listening. With under-threes and especially under-twos, your contribution is often to comment on what the child is doing or to voice out loud your contribution to this play or your visual search.

- Young children extend their own spoken vocabulary from experience with familiar adults who regularly add their words to name what a baby or toddler is currently holding or gazing towards.

- It works well sometimes to repeat what the child has said and extend a little. You say a word correctly as you reply, but do not make the child re-say it. You add a little – a few words, a short sentence – then pause and look expectant.

- You will steadily have longer, more complex conversations with articulate older twos and threes. The articulate threes and the over threes will be equal partners and will often lead the conversational direction.

- Young children build their vocabulary because familiar adults use 'new' words and phrases in a meaningful context. Children can make sense of the word and often choose to use it relatively soon, see the examples on page 21 and 34.

Attentive early years practitioners will recall previous conversations and shared experiences. When you know individual children, their further questions or comments do not appear to be from nowhere. You will grasp the link, although not always straightaway, because young children do not always give you a recap. You can get your bearings with a friendly question like "are we talking about...?" or even, "I'm a bit lost about what you mean by...please give me a clue". Your own strategy of recall and connection will often guide the child. For instance, when you return to a conversation you may need to make a link like "do you remember when we...? Well, I've found out about...". It is likely that children will follow your model and make it easier for you to make the thinking jump with them.

Shared: there are at least two partners in this communication and there is definitely a give-and-take between the adult and child(ren). The flow of SST is not exclusively about adult-led activities and it certainly is not about a set of questions that practitioners prepared earlier. The original EPPE research focused on how attentive early years practitioners came alongside young children in their child-initiated activities. However, the same sensitivity to your own adult communication will be very supportive of those times when you have initiated, and maybe led, an experience for children. Your

communication which supports SST will be part of how helpful adults welcome the situation when young children themselves mentally and physically seize a good idea and take it off in their chosen direction.

Thinking: here the experience is thoughtful, for both parties. SST is not about adults setting the agenda and leading children all the time. Practitioners will often be provoked to rethink and will certainly learn something new about this child or very small group. Child and adult thinking may be done out loud in words or through actions relevant to the current, shared enterprise. Sometimes, you will say as much as the child with whom you are talking. However, the measure of close adult involvement is not based on quantity of talking time. Sometimes, practitioners listen to a child's conversation, or the exchange between two or three children, for more of the time than they add a comment themselves. You learn by close attention and can better judge what you could offer in the future.

Look closer: Making marmalade
It is important to realise that sustained shared thinking accompanies an experience in which children and

adults are actively involved. SST is not about pre-planned communication or organised question-and-answer sessions. Garfield reception team place a high value on planning but they focus on the short term and being responsive to children's passion to find out or do something really interesting today. During the morning of my day visit, one child had expressed an interest in making marmalade and several children immediately agreed this idea was a really good project. The children in Garfield are keen cooks. They have a dedicated cooking area, with ingredients in a small fridge. Children are welcome to start cooking – the only ground rule is a maximum of two children at a time. Some children follow the recipes in their laminated book and others opt for creative baking – like Jasmin, see page 21.

The marmalade team said they needed a recipe and went with the adult to search the internet on the setting's computer. They found and printed a recipe and then discussed the ingredients. Some needed to be bought, so an adult went out with the children to the local shops. In the afternoon they set up everything on an indoor table and the group set to work cutting up the fruit with an adult. There was continued conversation about the recipe and the need to check, along with more general enjoyable chatting. The recipe required water so there was a discussion about, "how are we going to measure the water?".

The hob within the kitchen area of the reception class was temporarily out of order so the children and two adults set off with their ingredients – now in two large saucepans – to use the cooker in the school staff room. Once there, the children explained to the few teachers present what they were doing and why they needed to use this cooker. One adult did the stirring on the hob but the children remained close enough to see what was happening, to comment, question and be part of the adding of further ingredients. Once the mixture was bubbling, it was left with a teacher in the staff room who had promised to keep an eye on it.

The children returned to their reception class area. A discussion followed with one of the adults about what they could do with the pile of orange and lemon peel. They agreed to put it in the compost bin. Later in the come-together group time at the end of the day, the children heard that the cooked marmalade was now cooling in the staff room. They were invited to discuss what next. The children said the plan was to eat the marmalade as soon as possible and the general view was that they would need bread. Their teacher agreed he would buy fresh bread on his way into school tomorrow.

The intellectual and emotional challenge to adults is to tune-in to the understanding of very young children, whose limited knowledge gives them a fresh outlook and the motivation to ask intriguing questions. A further challenge to adults is to recognise those queries, and the desire to learn more, when babies and very young children cannot yet put their wondering into recognisable words. The EPPE research did not include any under twos and most children observed were at least three years old. However, babies and toddlers clearly do think, wonder and pose non-verbal questions to familiar adults. You just have to watch what they do. As their spoken language develops then those words are a help for adults to understand the thinking and relaxed young children often voice what they are doing and what has caught their attention.

Look closer: Sustained shared thinking with very young children

There were many times during my visit to Kennet Day Nursery when children, even young ones, explored actively without needing an adult companion. But there were also examples when an adult's presence made a real difference.

In Minnows (the base room of babies and toddlers) a young girl of 17 months and a boy of 15 months were interested in the little house and play figures. This age group are often starting to show elements of pretend play but are unlikely to initiate sequences. The practitioner was close to the toddlers, at their level, and completely followed their expressed interests. She watched what they did and commented briefly on the play. An 11-month-old joined them and watched whilst cuddling up to the adult.

The 15-month-old asked the names of items he did not know, including the little merry-go-round in the house. The practitioner answered each of his questions. She also responded immediately to how the toddlers wanted to play. One toddler pressed the button that worked the telephone in the house and she initiated a short and simple pretend telephone conversation and the toddlers joined in the exchange.

Building the train track

In Start Point Sholing Anna and Jon, both young three-year-olds, were keen to build a train track on the floor. A practitioner remained close to the children, watching and responding promptly to their particular interests.

Jon was especially keen to create a raised section in the track for a bridge. The practitioner suggested that maybe they could use a wooden block or large Duplo. Perhaps they could go to where the blocks were stored in the room and 'measure' some blocks against the track items that needed to fit. Both Jon and Anna showed enthusiasm for this idea and, by trial and error, identified a small block that would work. The practitioner commented: "It was worth searching to find something".

Then the track fell apart. The practitioner leaned forward and said: "I can see what's happening. When you moved that bit, the bridge fell apart". The children welcomed her help – but not taking over – as they worked to reconnect the sections of track. The practitioner continued to sit with the children as they tested their track, with the now secure bridge, and moved their train successfully onto the bridge. Jon pointed and the practitioner sounded as pleased as he looked when she said: "Yes, it's up on top, isn't it!" and Jon soon echoed, "Up on top!" as another train made the bridge crossing.

The practitioner remained a partner in the play, talking about "ideas that might work" and asking "what do we need to do?", rather than directing these very young children when their bridge enterprise went temporarily awry.

Of course you cannot plan what young children will think, no more than you can plan in advance what they will learn from any given experience. You can plan to provide a timing for the day or session that leaves scope for thinking time. You can avoid filling a day so full of planned activities that adults feel they have to keep moving children from one activity or part of the daily schedule to another. Best early years practice is to create a learning environment in which it is easy, and welcomed, for children to return to the same activity, area or resource after some thinking time. You can sometimes comment on what you notice they have changed in their approach: "I can see/ hear you've been thinking about..." or "now that's a new way of doing...your brain has been busy". You can also model what thinking is like by sometimes voicing your train of thought, or the options you are considering.

Attentive early years practitioners also support the process of sustained shared thinking by helping, as Marion Dowling expresses the concept, to make children's thinking visible. This concept is similar to the ideas from the Reggio Emilia early years centres of making children's learning visible. Sometimes that means adults need to capture the good ideas, or ideas in progress, in some kind of record, shared with children. This record of thinking may take the form of a temporary plan, documentation in a child's individual book or portfolio, or a wall display that grows over time and is directly interesting to many children.

Look closer: Making children's thinking visible
Children in Garfield reception class start by planning their day. Jasmin (one of the focus children for the week) sat at the front of the group with the practitioner and he invited: "Can you talk us through what you did?". Jasmin explained how she had made a cake yesterday and her words were supported by a series of photos projected onto the screen. Jasmin then outlined her plan for today, which was to organise a party. The practitioner made written and drawn notes on his clipboard, as Jasmin went through what was needed for a party. Other children contributed ideas about food (the centrepiece would be Jasmin's cake), music and other forms of entertainment. The discussion also determined where the party would take place – in one of the outdoor spaces – and Jasmin's chosen companions to help her set up the event.

Jasmin left, holding the clipboard, along with her party team and another practitioner. They organised seating outdoors, using wooden blocks and I joined them mid-morning when the food and drink had been enjoyed and

Links to your practice

How do you support young children to make their thinking visible and show your respect for that process? You might:

■ Scribe what children want to be able to recall later, whether the focus is a plan of action or a story that will later be developed or acted out for the key group.

■ Write words and short phrases but also little drawings that will help young children to make sense of their sheet. You hand over the clipboard or notes to the child.

■ Add children's opinions and expressed thoughts to a wall display or in their personal record book. You make sure to put their actual words in quotation marks or maybe in a speech bubble, when they are on a wall display.

You always ensure that the photos and written explanations – for a display or personal record – are chosen because they directly reflect what interested the children. Any kind of record needs to grow over time; there should be no sense of pressure that anything must be finished quickly. The main point is to show how something has evolved – as the consuming interest of one or two children or a shared enterprise in which many of the group were involved.

the group had moved into the music. At one point there was some tightly organised dancing and a team member gave me the back story. The children had immediately recognised the song. Back in the winter (my visit was in April) a different child had been keen on dancing and her plan was that she and her chosen friends would choreograph a dance routine to a Beyoncé track. They had organised the entire routine and performed it to the primary school in assembly. This was the track and the children went into the dance routine.

. . . .

Deep interest in tube trains

Kashif (just four-years-old) started to travel by underground train when his family moved out of walking distance from the Randolph Beresford Early Years Centre. Kashif soon became very interested in the tube trains and chose to draw the trains and other elements of stations, like the escalator.

His drawings became more and more detailed. With his agreement, Kashif's key person started a wall display of his research about the underground. His drawings were joined by photos of the underground system, downloaded with help from the Internet. Kashif became interested in the sequence of stations that he and his parent travelled through each day and asked his key

person to work with him on a large chart to show the journey. Kashif told her the names of the stations and she wrote them on the chart. But soon Kashif was keen to produce his own versions of the station names. Other children have also become interested in drawing trains.

Leading a child-focused approach

This section does not exclusively speak to early years practitioners who manage the different types of group provision and their colleagues who form the senior team, many of the points are equally relevant to childminders: you lead yourself in a child-focused approach (if that does not seem an odd concept).

Senior practitioners and those working as sole practitioners, need to be familiar with the details of the early years framework that applies to your part of the UK. In terms of the EYFS, managers must take a lead for their staff in understanding what is required and, just as much, the considerable amount that is open to your professional judgement. You need to know good early years practice thoroughly in order to challenge – in a professional way – an inspector or any other official visitor – who expects to see lesson plans or other approaches which would be poor EYFS practice. The Ofsted website (page 37) makes public the guidance that inspectors must follow and the most recent edition (2012) applied to the revised EYFS. Pages 10-11 are especially relevant to this section and start with a valuable reminder that best practice is never about a 'race' towards the early learning goals.

Early years practitioners are expected to make observations, to reach considered judgements from those observations and to plan ahead in a flexible way – so that children have a breadth of experiences. However, neither the previous, nor the revised EYFS, nor the Ofsted Inspectorate seek to determine the exact way in which practitioners should observe, record or plan ahead. The inspectors are expected to be alert for examples of self-chosen play and – again very valuable – directed not to expect written plans for everything. However, managers and practitioners have a responsibility to be ready to talk about aspects of their good practice and be able to explain choices, decisions and how your approach works to benefit children.

Planning that pays off for children

The more adults prepare activities in advance, the less children have a shared ownership and feeling of engagement in the enterprise. The most effective adult-led or initiated experiences have plenty of scope for children to determine how the details evolve over time. Planning does matter and adult thoughtfulness is part of best early years practice. But the big question is what does that word 'planning' actually mean to practitioners? What should planning mean, if early childhood is to be an interesting time, full of genuine learning and

welcome memories for young children – and the adults who share their days?

A developmentally appropriate perspective on planning has to be based fully within a personal relationship with children, and their families – the reason why this book is grounded within the EYFS strand of Positive Relationships.

■ A good rule of thumb is that it should never be difficult for practitioners to complete the sentence: "Today (or this week) has been different because…" with a change that has come about because of what babies or children did, said or requested this morning, yesterday or last week.

■ Try this question applied to your own practice. If you struggle for an answer, then it is most likely a sign that you, and your colleagues in a team, are over-organising children's days in advance.

■ Wise planning for, and with, young children has never been about written plans, established well in advance and perhaps even drafted by somebody who has never met these individual children.

- The measure of worthwhile planning is whether it directly benefits young children, not whether it reassures adults or satisfies strangers who do not even know these young boys and girls.

- Some published or Internet sources promote ready done plans, claiming that these will enable early years practitioners to generate evidence for the inspector. The only evidence these layouts generate is of adults who have lost their way and are not paying attention to the actual children in front of them.

Each setting mentioned in this book took planning seriously. But every team worked on a short-term planning perspective in terms of experiences for the children. Even with the four-year-olds, the planning that affected what was likely to happen each day went no further than two to three weeks ahead at most. In each provision, any longer-term adult planning focused on improving the indoor and outdoor learning environment – always still with a close eye and ear on how children used resources at that moment in time. This longer-term perspective was also relevant for developing the team's approach to planning as a whole, identifying the continuing professional development of team members and joint ventures between the setting and other professionals, such as the Sightlines outdoors projects I visited in Tyneside (see page 15 and 29).

Look closer: Reception class at Garfield Children's Centre

Both the reception and nursery class follow the same child-focused approach to observation and planning, built around three focus children each week. I spent most of my visit with reception and the Garfield approach is striking, because this way of working is often a challenge to maintain in that last year of the EYFS. The centre is part of Garfield Primary School, whose head is fully supportive of the early years team. At the time of my visit, the Year 6 teacher was planning to introduce a similar approach for planning with her class.

The process starts on a Friday when a sheet goes home with the names of next week's focus children, inviting their family to describe the current interests of their son or daughter, any recent family events and any subjects on which their child has been keen to ask questions. Each reception teacher, supported by their colleague in that class, plans immediately on the basis of this child's expressed interests (see the examples on page 8 and 21). The longest gap is until tomorrow, for events that need a bit of prior organisation.

Each of the focus children is featured on the special board in reception class. Their chosen interests and experiences are documented on the board, building up over the week. What has been learned from each child's

special week forms part of their ongoing personal record, in which the team continue to highlight the developing skills and next steps for this individual boy or girl.

The Garfield team have put considerable thought into the resourcing of the indoor and outdoor learning environment of the reception class. The focus children have the full attention of an adult for periods of time. However, this quality time is part of a day in which all the practitioners are highly available to children. My visit was full of observations of adults who followed the interests of all the children and not exclusively the focus children of the week.

The approach was trialled in reception and had run for just over a year when I visited. Previously, the team had made plans for the following week on the basis of the current week. However, they found that the gap was enough that individual interests had already changed. The reception team have found that the new approach has enabled them to focus much more closely on children's interests. They have stopped planning any additional adult-initiated or adult-led activities. There is plenty of time and they use it to work directly with what has intrigued children that day. The team was very aware that spontaneous conversations and play were the best opportunities for sustained shared thinking (see page 18 for more on SST).

. . . .

Ladybirds Pre-School

The team work with the Southampton Learning Story approach (www.southamptonchildcare.org.uk/workforce) and build up documentation over time. The key person keeps the records of their key children. However, the team follows a pattern of focusing on a small number of named children in each session. Each day everyone is keeping a special alert eye and ear for those children and noting down observations on white sticky labels, which the key person organises into the children's individual folders. These observations lead to discussion and thought about the next steps in the development of this child, but they also regularly lead to planning for experiences and providing resources that other children will enjoy.

The pre-school garden has a digging area – a space dedicated to digging in the earth, which is separate from their vegetable garden. On my visit I watched two boys busy in the earth, covering up the wooden pig that sits in the middle. They then cleared the earth off the pig and started to fill buckets "for my castle". They made an earth castle which then collapsed. Among the tools they were using were two metal trowels. A practitioner explained to me that one boy had seen a real bricklayer working in his family life and had brought his enthusiasm about brick laying into his pre-school. The team had bought proper trowels to add to the digging area and took care to explain about safe use of this kind of tool. They had also provided a system of string and two metal pegs – for lining up bricks. The team leader was currently seeking a local bricklayer who could come into Ladybirds and give a demonstration to the children.

The Ladybirds team plans ahead in this way – there are no adult led topics. In terms of special resources or experiences they plan no further than one week ahead, guided by observed interests of children. The only exception is when organising a special experience which will take a bit more time and also to take the opportunity of a small number of festivals within the rhythm of the year.

> Promoting active first-hand experiences

The National Strategies guidance for early years consultants (DCSF, 2010) stressed that adult-led, planned learning opportunities should be in response to what practitioners have observed of children's interests. There is a clear focus on the responsibility of practitioners to provide "worthwhile real life experiences" and "first-hand experiences to explore and discover" (appearing in particular on pages 9, 23 and 24). This heightened awareness of first-hand experiences has grown in EYFS guidance since the publication of the statutory framework and practice guidance in 2007/8. There was a single direct reference, on page 78 in the 2008 Practice Guidance, although much of the descriptive material implied a focus on first-hand experiences The Foundation Phase for 3-7s in Wales (2008) places the concept as central to their curriculum framework with, "First-hand experiences allow children to develop an understanding of themselves and the world in which they live" (page 4).

It is necessary to explore the nature of real life and first-hand experiences (Rich et al., 2005, 2008). This powerful source of learning for children is a rather alien concept for practitioners who have been bombarded with second-hand, pre-packaged activities in the name of early learning – and in some cases keeping the inspector happy with cross referenced evidence.

So what are the main characteristics of first-hand experiences?

- Children can literally get their hands on materials. They can move around a collection of shells; they are not faced with a photocopied sheet of images. They can take their shoes and socks off and feel the sand on their toes (page 13). They make the marmalade (page 19) and the jam tarts (page 26). Children can use all their senses, with the friendly support of an adult who ensures that very young children are safe, as can older children whose learning disabilities mean they are less aware of hazards.

- The experience is drawn from real life and any adult-led/initiated activity starts with the real thing. Practitioners do not start with an activity sheet about how to make a pretend tropical fish tank. You would reach this focused activity only from a genuine wish from children to make their own tank, with all the trimmings. You lead and support this kind of experience with the real thing – like visiting somewhere with an actual fish tank – or you get as close as possible to the real thing (see building the volcano on page 26).

- Resources and any events are authentic. If there is any pretending to be done, it is started by children. You go out looking for real bugs and other little creatures – see the example below. You plant real flowers and vegetables, as did all the settings which I visited. You go out and about in the local neighbourhood and build on what children can see, hear, ask about and recall. You may need to prepare some places and people to be ready for young children when you visit, but then you want children to be shown how things work and properly.

- Experiences are not unnecessarily simplified or produced in children's versions. Gardening implements and woodworking tools need to be the right size for little hands. But otherwise young children need the real thing, which will work and that will usually not be plastic. Children can cook with many of the same implements as adults and they do not need kiddie versions in bright primary colours or plastered with logos. If children are absorbed in counting and organising, they will do that with a wide range of materials. They will use their emergent mathematical skills to a chosen purpose. They do not need adults to buy special sets of plastic counting frogs or any other budget-draining materials aggressively marketed in the name of early learning.

■ Technology is used for a good reason, such as searching with four- or five-year-olds for a recipe or finding out information that children want to know right now, and it is not available here in a book. DVDs can be the only way to see and makes sense of habitats and creatures you cannot visit. Otherwise, it makes no sense for adults or children to be working on screen or printing off worksheets. Nor should young children be offered a virtual reality on the screen, because practitioners think it is too cold, hot, wet, dry, snowy, windy, sunny or whatever, outside in the real natural world.

Look closer: Building a volcano

I visited Randolph Beresford Centre in the second week of the summer term of 2010. Over the Easter holiday the volcano in Iceland had erupted. The nursery school team were ready to seize this real news opportunity, and the children were aware of the event from the news coverage.

In the first week of term children had enjoyed adult-led experiences of creating volcanoes with a mixture of vinegar and bicarbonate of soda in plastic bottles. Volcano creation had extended over that week and by my visit there was a permanent volcano feature within the outdoor sand area. A black tuff spot included sand and stones. It was surrounded by laminated photos of the actual volcano, along with photos of children and the volcanoes they made the previous week. Several children were keen to explain to me what was in this special area and what they had done. They understood about the real event: what volcanoes did and what the hot lava was like. They were also enthusiastic about the yellow and other coloured stones that were part of what their volcano, like a real one, had thrown out.

A practitioner explained to me that they were about to make the volcano creation resources available for children to brew their own. There was also a plan for adults and children to take the equipment on their next trip to their local woodland copse (part of the Forest School initiative in the centre).

Making jam tarts

You lead as an adult when this experience will benefit from your taking a more active guiding role. You have something valuable to offer to the children now, in this context; your contribution will make a positive difference. Helpful early years practitioners do not take over play or conversation which children are able and keen to direct themselves.

Start Point Sholing Nursery has a proper working kitchen, accessed through a room divider and gate at child height. Over the day of my visit, small groups of three of four children at a time enjoyed making jam tarts with a practitioner, not the same adult each time. Batches were cooked and enjoyed throughout the day.

I watched the last afternoon group, which happened to be four boys. Each child had their own board, rolling pin and pastry cutter. The practitioner gave the children scope for decisions, within the practical focus of eventually making tarts which would be edible. He was patient, reminding children of the technique for mixing, rolling and cutting and of the steps within the task. He commented for instance on a shape in the tart tin: "That one's a bit small". This was a wise comment, because the pastry shape would not have taken the jam and made a viable tart. The practitioner left the final decision up to the young cooks. He also showed the boys how to place the jam accurately in the pastry tart shape. Again this was wise guidance, as anyone will know who has had tarts stick completely to the baking tray, because the jam has run over the edge of the pastry.

Going on the bug hunt

The learning journey is a personal one. Children may share common interests and joint enterprises, but they will learn something different from the same experience. In Kennet Day Nursery the older toddlers and twos went outside on a search for little creatures. Accompanied by several practitioners, the children carried binoculars or small wooden frames with safety glass in different tints. The planning for this adult-initiated experience was simple: the binoculars and wooden frames were ready for children to take out. The experience was gently led by practitioners who were as interested as the children in what they could find, or what happened if you looked through the tinted frames.

They started with the patch of small purple flowers flourishing in the grass. Children chose to look through the tinted glass and adults commented, as appropriate, for instance: "It's all gone blue". Some children chose to look through the binoculars. The main practitioner leading the experience got very close and used small twigs to push the grass apart as they searched for little creatures. Some children also got themselves twigs. A search for snails came up with more snail shells than occupied ones. But one baby snail was discovered.

This experience continued for about 20-25 minutes as children and adults moved in a relaxed way between

Child-Initiated Learning

parts of the garden. At each point children and one or two adults were crouched down, with bent knees looking very carefully at the ground. During the snail search, one practitioner encouraged careful looking by behaving in that way herself, as well as posing open questions like "what can we see?/what's here?/let's have a look" and "I wonder if we can find...". She also added her own comments, including: "It's a pretend centipede" when a child found a hard plastic creature which had been lost in the foliage. When a real beetle was discovered, she coaxed it onto her twig and showed it to the children.

Experiences that are led by adults for younger children can, in time, become child-initiated as children understand enough to organise themselves. The three- and four-year-olds in Kennet are keen to do their own independent bug hunting. That afternoon I watched three girls searching out creatures across the different sections of their garden. They chose to take laminated sheets hanging from an outdoor structure and fix them to clipboards. They collected felt tip pens and set off on the hunt. At various stages they returned to their chosen seating area to compare what they had, or had not, found. They were also interested to show practitioners, and myself as a visitor, what they had found and what they were still seeking from their sheet.

today or over this week. Your continuous assessment is best seen as a continued alertness to what children are doing, with whom and with what.

The Sightlines Initiative team, led by Robin Duckett, act as facilitators in the regular team discussions which are part of the joint projects with settings like Stocksfield Nursery and Skerne Park Reception Class, whose visits to the woodland I was able to join. Think about the questions below, which I have expressed in my own words, and how they could guide your thoughtful practice.

- The Sightlines approach is to focus on what exactly has interested children: what is it about aspects of the woodland and how children have used that environment? The aim is to notice in full what children have chosen to do today. But you also look through their eyes to understand what made the digging so important, or how different individuals managed their own uncertainty as they moved into less familiar parts of the environment.

- The aim is that nursery and reception practitioners consider what underlies the current interests. what exactly fascinates the children, what matters to them? These are consistent themes within children's engagement; it is not a case of trying to fit or create an adult-led topic.

Observation to work alongside children's interests

Both the 2008 and revised EYFS Statutory Framework stress the importance of observation-led planning and continuous or regular assessment. Both these concepts could have done with more immediate explanation in the 2008 edition, in response to the high level of anxiety within the early years workforce. Neither of these elements of best practice are about piles of paperwork, nor observations cross-referenced to the Development Matters materials. The first and revised version (Early Education, 2012) of this information were neither of them designed as a tracking tool. Managers may still need to guide less experienced practitioners to know that none of these developmental descriptive statements are statutory. The only required focus for observation is the details of the early learning goals – much reduced in the 2012 EYFS – for the end of the early childhood stage.

The point about alert adult observation is that you notice recurring play patterns and persistent interests of individual children or small groups who spend time together. The practical concept of 'next steps' or 'what next?' planning rests on your awareness of what engages children now. Your short-term plans have to connect with what you have noticed

- The aim in such discussion is for practitioners to feel comfortable about personal observations and feelings about what was happening. Some advice about observation is critical of what are viewed as subjective comments. In fact, practitioners' supported opinions are crucial: the approach of "I think …" or "I feel…" but always accompanied with the essential "because…" from what they have seen and heard whilst with the children.

- How can the adults best act to support that interest – what the Sightlines team describes as 'picking up on the children's ideas and running with them'? How do you guide without taking over? How are you a helpful adult companion, but avoid stepping in to do things or help when children could work it out for themselves, or show each other. Direct proposals from adults about possible actions are fine, so long as they are grounded in reasons linked with the children's interests and enterprises.

- Each team gives time to discuss what most interested children and how that interest could be supported in nursery or reception (see the example on page 29). How do you support genuine connections between what happens in the woodland and back at base in nursery or reception? Part of this bridge is talking about the experience with the children themselves, what Sightlines call "invitations to recall", which are part of natural conversation between children and adults who are also part of the outdoor visits.

Look closer: Kennet Day Nursery

The team at Kennet Day Nursery focus on noticing and following what has engaged children's interests today and this week. Like many early years settings, Kennet has many children who attend part-time and practitioners need their concise professional notes to make the links of interest for the days when those children are in nursery again.

Practitioners working with the under-threes go with what babies, toddlers and twos wish to do today (see the examples on page 15 and 20). The team are also alert for books that have especially caught the very young children's attention. In the early part of the year a number of children were especially keen on play evolving from *The Gruffalo* (Donaldson, Macmillan, 1999). At another time, their wish to hear *Handa's Surprise* (Browne, Walker, 2006) many times was a good reason to provide a wide array of actual fruit. During the period of my visits, several children had shown an interest in rockets and diggers and for that reason there were a range of relevant titles in the book corner.

A flexible rolling plan for the over-threes starts with experiences that practitioners plan to make available at the beginning

Food for thought

In a joint project with Walkergate Early Years Centre, Sightlines Initiative (2008) describe the sense of 'quiet companionship' with children. Valuable adults listen, watch with children and do not rush to fill silences with comments and questions.

The adult role in observation was to keep open-eyed and never assume that the adult agenda was the same as that of the children, nor that the adult assumptions or conclusions were necessarily the more accurate. The point of observation was to contribute to children's experience on the basis of improved adult understanding. The point is well put by, "We learned to use observation as a form of companionship rather than merely a means of assessment".

of the week, based on the events of last week. These special possibilities are in addition to a well-resourced indoor and outdoor learning environment. These opportunities are based on what has been noticed from a specific observation or an observed continuing area of interest for an individual child or group of play companions – see the cardboard box example below. The planner continues to be completed through the week on the basis of what actually happens. Everything is not written on the plan; practitioners are swift to respond to child-initiated events like the drummers who became the plumbers, page 3.

A small group of three- and four-year-olds were keen on play with large cardboard boxes. A practitioner explained to me how they had observed these children had a long-term interest in the schema of enclosure. The adults had secured a good supply of boxes. Over the afternoon these children enthusiastically followed this interest, organising themselves and fetching other resources as and when they needed something extra. They played inside and outside the boxes, decided they wanted to draw on the boxes, went inside and fetched a range of felt tip pens. It is fully understood in Kennet Day Nursery that children can move resources to where they wish to use them – indoors and outdoors. One boy decided he wanted to cut and fetched scissors, which he made available for the other children to use as well. Another boy chose a puppet from those in the black tuff spot outside, took it into his box plus some material. He made an enclosed den with the cardboard box and played with the puppet inside.

Later that afternoon I saw three girls and one boy still absorbed with their highly decorated boxes. The boxes were now mainly very flat, but two of the children were sitting happily in their personal box, legs inside the cardboard and drawing on the outside. Decoration with the felt tips continued, along with careful and purposeful cutting of small sections of the cardboard, which were then laid carefully on the side or slipped back into the box.

In Dragonflies (the three- and four-year-olds), the team look ahead no more than two weeks ahead in terms of plans for key person group time. Even then, a group activity, planned on the basis of individual interests, is still flexible in the light of children's reactions on the actual day. I watched as one key group became steadily less interested in the books shared by their key person and more engaged by the cooking of the nearby group. The practitioner noticed, asked the children if they would rather make chocolate Rice Krispies® cakes like the other group and responded to the clear "Yes please".

This example highlights that it is good practice to respond to children's clearly expressed preferences. A wise practitioner knows not to insist on continuing an activity when young children have become enthused with an alternative that will be equally rich in potential learning.

Your awareness of children's next steps in any area of development can be applied thoughtfully to another activity. Your awareness of children's next steps in any area of development can be applied thoughtfully to different activity from the one you planned. In this example, for instance, any realistic hopes for learning around Communication, Language and Literacy from enjoying the books were just as likely to be supported by the buzz of conversation about cooking and following the recipe.

Best practice is that children's personal learning journeys are captured as they unfold today, this week, over this month – so there is no problem in allowing time and space for child-initiated play. They are busy learning – you just have to notice what is happening today and this week. Each of the settings I visited had personal documentation for each individual child and that detailed record grew over time, with direct contributions from children as they developed and a welcome for families to add to the record. Practitioners kept the records of their key children but with contributions from colleagues who had made spontaneous observations and/or shared in conversation the highlights of play and conversation with individual children.

The aim of any documentation has to be that it works to show children's personal learning journey. Photos, written observations or items that children want included are also shown with an explanation of how and why this event or experience was of importance to this child and maybe also their chosen companions. The documentation was linked with areas of learning and development but any connections emerged from the observation. Incidents were not slotted into single headings from the six EYFS areas. Descriptions were individual to the child and the experience, not quotations lifted straight from EYFS statutory or guidance materials.

Look closer: Observations that enable making connections

Best early years practice is to make it easy for children to make connections between experiences and for their interests and passions to be welcome. The reception team of Skerne Park Primary School have changed their approach to planning through an active shift to building on children's interests, in particular from the regular woodland trips.

Meaningful connections for children go in both directions. On the morning of my visit a group of several girls and boys spent a considerable amount of the morning digging for buried treasure. Wielding their spades with great enthusiasm, they created a substantial hole and then filled it in again, using the earth but also bricks and other materials that are in the woodland space. (The area used to be part of the railway and the land is full of left behind materials.) At an interim point, they were also burying treasure: twigs, pine cones and other woodland items. The back story is that this group of children has a long running fascination with digging, finding treasure and pirates. This consuming interest seems to date back to last year when the Skerne Park nursery and reception had a special event about pirates. Some children always now dig as part of their woodland visit. The pirates and buried treasure theme generated a great deal of spontaneous conversation – where the treasure might be, what would be buried, how you found treasure again if you buried it (making an X marks the spot). The details evolved into a narrative that one adult wrote down for the children as their chosen story that needed to be captured and not forgotten. The pirate play continued back at reception class into the afternoon and various characters developed their narrative of buried treasure and other events out in the garden.

I had the opportunity to spend time in Skerne Park reception class in the afternoon. The reception teacher and her team changed their approach to planning this year to build from observations of children's expressed interests. The two main created corners inside the reception class are a den and a theatre.

- The den and den building emerged from the fascination of several children for building dens in the woodland. Other children have become very interested in making other structures from materials found in the wood. Earlier in the year, a large stick man was started in the woods and brought back to reception where it was completed and is still displayed in the classroom.

- The theatre evolved from taking the children to see Aladdin the previous Christmas. The children wanted their own theatre, they built it with adult support in the classroom and it is still there and frequently used for impromptu shows.

Since the Autumn, the reception team have stopped using pre-planned topics or adult-determined role play boxes of materials. Their observations have generated plenty of evidence about the children's learning by the approach of building on their interests. A more formal approach to early writing has been replaced with time, resources and encouragement for children to use their emergent writing skills for their own enterprises. The reception team have established that this group of children has advanced further in their literacy than the group of last year who were given structured group teaching in the Sounds and Letters programme.

Writing and drawing materials are taken with the children into the woodland. During the morning I had observed many children who picked up clipboards and pencils regularly. One boy spent time up in the climbing tree, making drawings of trees and other parts of the woodland from different perspectives. In the afternoon, several children were organising their drawings or items they had brought back. One boy was keen to take his teacher

through his set of drawings and explain them all to her in detail. One boy spent some time carefully making labels for his woodland finds. Two girls and a boy had created their own register at the beginning of the afternoon and were checking and ticking people but also a range of creatures. I commented to the boy: "Are you ticking people off?" and he replied, very logically: "No, I'm ticking up."

Generous table and wall space in the reception class is assigned to the woodland experience. Children were busy on the table, organising out of choice what they had done in the morning. One boy was building a house for his 'family' of snail shells that he had carried back.

The children were keen to explain to me as a visitor what the photos showed. They talked at length about when their parent(s) saw the woodland during the special family trip, which photos were from the 'new' camp that I had visited and which from 'old camp', their base last year. They also explained special places, like how one tree was for a while known as the Leopard Tree, which has been the spot to look out for (imaginary!) fierce animals.

A welcoming learning environment

In a well-resourced learning environment, and a day that has child-friendly routines, it should be relatively easy to notice what engages individual babies, toddlers and young children. So, it is important to reflect on possible reasons, if any readers are thinking they observe individual children yet have not identified any obvious personal interests.

- Do some children in your setting really have no interests? What makes you think that? Bear in mind that interest can be shown in different ways – see the discussion about schemas on page 12.

- Are they just quiet, watching until they make a choice? Or do they move around a lot and not settle in your view? How old is this child and in what ways does his or her key person come alongside the play, the movement or the watching?

- How do you judge interest? Does a child have to play for a long time or use resources in a particular way? How does your learning environment work – can children usually move resources to where they are needed – in the child's view?

- Is it an adult problem that children appear to be 'doing the same thing non-stop'? The power of play across childhood is that children can repeat broad patterns of engagement with the same resources. When practitioners observe what is actually happening, you will often see distinct variations around a central theme that matters to the children.

- Is there a possibility that children are expressing clear interests, but that their focus is not judged worthy of respect by the adults? See the discussion on page 34 about lively physical play and pretend play themes.

- What kind of experience have children had so far? Have they spent a very great deal of time in front of a television or computer screen, so that their habits are already very passive? Are they disconcerted by a play-rich environment and need their key person to be a friendly play partner?

- Is the child finding it hard to cope with the nature of the environment? Is the atmosphere overwhelming – very noisy and full of bustle? Do you need to create quieter, smaller spaces, more peaceful times?

- Wide scope for choosing should not be a burden to a child. Some children, and not only those on the autistic spectrum, sometimes welcome less upon choice and an adult who is a close play companion.

All the settings I visited had thought carefully about the learning environment they offered children. Each setting looked different but these were the important shared aspects.

- Practitioners had reflected, and continued to discuss in the team, how best to use their indoor and outdoor spaces. They all operated free-flow between indoors and the garden area. Settings for whom free flow is genuinely not possible (and I know this can be the situation) need to ensure that the day or session is organised to give a generous amount of time outdoors.

- Planning effort had gone into the physical layout of the learning environment. Different types of storage systems, with clear picture and written labelling, enabled young children to access materials and, with help, put them back again.

- There were stores of open-ended materials and resources like blocks were provided in a generous amount. Tools, for instance for gardening, worked properly and were easily available. Resources were kept in good condition and, as appropriate, made available in ways that caught the attention.

- Teams used the space and spaces they had and thought about routes indoors and outdoors, so that children could move, with or without carrying resources, and not be forced to walk through other children busy on the floor or ground.

- Materials were collected together in areas in a way that made sense for their likely use. There was a workshop approach but the areas of interest were not rigidly maintained. It was understood that children took resources to where they needed them and were encouraged at tidy-up time to bring things back.

- There was open and unallocated space and the understanding that sometimes the best place for play was the floor or the ground. Indoor and outdoor spaces were created by visible boundaries, sometimes by storage systems, low room dividers and floor coverings. Each setting also had small cosy spaces, often with drapery, that were available for children to use however they wished, including just being restful.

Look closer: Making the most of spaces

Ladybirds Pre-School is on a primary school site and their outdoor space is a fenced section of playground. The basic area could be seen as unpromising. But the team has shown you can create an excellent outdoor environment by thinking about use of available space and leaving enough open space for children to move and organise themselves – see the milk crate examples on page 7.

They invested in a substantial outdoor storage facility and organised the storage with clear labelling. Children can

easily access resources and understand how to replace items at tidy-up time. Their large shed was designed with the assumption that resources would be removed and then the doors shut. The Ladybirds team noticed early on that children wanted to use the inside area. So the doors are now left open and chairs and table are set up in the available space inside the shed. The wooden petrol pumps, which had been set in the outside of the door were moved to the inside. So the shed is now a fully used facility, with the two doors held open, providing a full resource for play.

The outdoor area has dedicated space for wheeled vehicles, limited by visual boundaries created by cones and a step-a-log; dual purpose in that children can walk and balance at a low level. They also sometimes put up fabric to create a higher, floaty visual barrier, which often comes down to make props for the children's play.

There is also a general digging area, separate areas where the adults and children grow flowers and vegetables. Last year they harvested a range of vegetables. The team has a good relationship with the cook in the primary school, who cooked their vegetables so the children could enjoy the full cycle of planting, growing and eating. They have a small area covered with a piece of old carpet, which is their bug place. Children can at any time lift the carpet and check out what is happening below. They have a number of outdoor seating areas and one sheltered area with warm floor covering set up each day. Children

choose to spend time in this cosy outdoor space, taking with them whatever they wanted at the time.

The indoors environment has been created to offer larger and smaller spaces. Children can spread out on the floor with resources of their own choice. A well-resourced creative area was regularly used by children throughout the day and they were able to take resources elsewhere if they needed. The children called this area 'The Making Place', so the team changed the previous laminated sign to respect the children's choice. Storage units are used to create boundaries, so that children can build, enjoy books, sit and chat. A small, den-like cosy space has been made using a large mosquito net hanging from the ceiling, wooden edging to give a visual boundary and comfortable floor coverings. Ladybirds also has a development and movement area in which children can be physically very active – a similar initiative to Start Point Sholing, see the example on page 24.

Pleased to show everyone what we enjoy here

Part of a welcoming and interesting learning environment is that practitioners share documentation of what children have themselves judged to be well worth their time and energy. Teams should never feel they have to fill their walls with a display and good practice is to think about what you fix up and why.

Randolph Beresford is a large centre and the layout of the building offers many places for showing what children have done and their own chosen projects. The team use the walls in group rooms and the documentation evolves over time.

One group had become very interested in cooking over the previous term. The photos, brief written explanation and verbatim comments of children formed a detailed wall display. It was possible to follow how these three- and four-year-olds had spent time on actual cooking, how their interest has fed into their pretend play cooking in the home corner, with sand, water and salt resources. They had visited a local bakery and been able to see the details of how real bread was made. Back at the centre, they had made different kinds of bread themselves and the display offered to share their recipes. The wall display also had two envelope holders with sheets that parents were welcome to take: how to make play dough for pretend cooking and other play and an actual bread recipe.

The team also use the extensive walls of their long corridor as a means of communication for parents and other visitors. However, children often stop and look when they are using the corridor to move around the centre or during lunchtime, when they eat at tables set in the spaces along the corridor. Some examples include:

▨ A substantial display of children's drawings shows a range of children's personal creations and documents what they wished to say about their work – in actual words and written explanation by adults. Other, brief written explanations expressed the reasons – to fellow adults – why drawing is important and how it shows children's skills.

▨ Another display features photos of children, holding their favourite book and explanations of why they like this book in particular.

▨ The team make use of sequences of photos that tell the story of an experience, such as 'We have been exploring in the snow', 'Green room go gardening' and for local trips in the neighbourhood. The regular outings of small groups to a local woodland copse are also documented fully in an area dedicated to 'Our Forest School'.

A series of large, laminated books in the reception area of the centre are works in progress to be completed over a period of time. One shows 'Writing for a purpose' and includes photos, examples and explanations of meaningful mark making and emergent writing. The wall displays and large books are drafted in straightforward language and do not rest on listing quotations from the EYFS.

Respect for physically lively play

Early years practitioners can only support child-initiated learning when they show a genuine interest in, and respect for what interests children. All the settings I visited for this book had managers who valued energetic physical play for young children and had supported their team in discussion around acceptable risk, scope for adventure and any wise ground rules. In recent years I have talked with many other teams who have reorganised their planning towards generous scope for children's wish to be active in their play and to pursue their current interests, rather than have to sit 'nicely' for long stretches of time. Practitioners have observed the disappearance of 'behaviour problems' arising from ordinarily lively little boys. They also comment that 'boy-friendly' practice is in reality best early years practice; the changes benefit the girls just as much.

Look closer: Time to leap and climb

In Start Point Sholing, young children have considerable scope for using and practising their physical skills. Outdoors they are able to spend generous time climbing, clambering, riding, running. Practitioners respond with admiration when asked to "look!" and give a helping hand if one is wanted, for instance when a toddler wanted help to jump down from the climbing frame. Indoors, all the children have constant access to a physical movement area located in the day nursery space. This much used resource was created after training by Jabadao in the Southampton area. This area is contained by low room dividers and equipped with soft floor mats and large foam shapes.

In the morning I watched two and then three boys in sustained purposeful play in this area. They were engaging in rough and tumble and obviously, from their expressions and whoops, having a very good time. The team are consistent that such play is to be encouraged and the advantage of the movement area is that it is very unlikely that the children can hurt themselves. Also their lively physical play cannot spill into quieter play, where other children would not appreciate anyone wrestling over the top of them.

The boys were busy building simple structures with the foam shapes, including the means to climb up against the back wall. These large oblong wedges were about the same size as the children. They grappled with the shapes to get them in the right position and talked together about what they could do. Within the space there was a great deal of chosen vigorous movements: bending, rolling up their legs and pulling them in tight against their chest. In the afternoon I watched another group of boys (girls also accessed the area during the day). These boys were keen to build a bridge structure and cooperation was necessary, with comments between the boys like "you'll have to do it. I'm not strong enough" and "help me get it here". They used the bridge structure for slow climbing across from one side to another. Despite the boys' careful, slow movements, the bridge fell apart several times and they rebuilt it. After one dramatic disintegration, I said: "Oh, your bridge has collapsed!". One three-year-old seemed to like the phrase and the sound of the word 'collapse' and repeated it several times.

Teams in the settings I visited had also all resolved any concerns around superhero play and pretend weapons. Again this practice issue seems to catch the boys in particular when their passionate commitment to certain pretend play themes is deemed a problem by the adults. None of the settings I visited were overrun by boys and pretend weaponry; all the teams had ground rules of play shared with the children.

About three years ago the team at Kennet Day Nursery addressed the issues around superhero and weapon play. They took the view that this play should be given the same level of respect as any pretend play theme. The team had, like many other settings, previously actively discouraged this kind of play. They decided to invite parents of the three- and four-year-olds to a meeting to explain how they had reflected on the issue and had decided to stop saying 'no'. Like other settings who have taken this wise step, the Kennet team have found that this kind of pretend play has flourished with adult acceptance and is rich in imagination and communication. At a relatively early stage after the change, practitioners from Kingfishers (the 3-5s group) took children on a walking trip to the local market. The boys and girls chose lengths of material to buy from the stall. They brought the cloth back to nursery and cut out their own superhero capes. These simple props were used for a considerable length of time.

Look closer: The dragon story

The Ladybirds Pre-School team takes the line that superhero, monster and pretend weapon play should be welcomed as a rich source of children's chosen imaginative fantasy play themes. During the morning of my visit there was a long-running narrative led by four boys and joined by one practitioner in an active role, following the boys' lead. Other adults were drawn into the story at various points in the morning.

The narrative started as a dragon hunt. One boy was the dragon and wore a dragon head mask. The others were hunting him, armed with their pretend weapons. The practitioner asked: "What has the dragon done?".

The boys explained in an excited manner the dangers posed by this dragon and why it had to be caught and probably killed. The boy with the dragon head queried: "But dragons never die" and there was some discussion around this possibility. The practitioner noticed and mentioned that the dragon's shadow, visible on the ground, was "a bit scary". The dragon catchers headed off in a boat (the permanent climbing structure in the garden), with a very long cardboard tube which was initially a weapon and then became a pole to move the boat along.

After about five minutes of the boat trip, the now three dragon fighters drew the adult's attention to the shadows. They were all intrigued and the practitioner offered whether they wanted to chalk around their shadow outline. This suggestion was accepted warmly and the dragon hunt was postponed for enthusiastic chalking.

The boys and some other children then returned to their travels and the climbing frame became a plane taking them to Never Never Land. The adult asked if anyone had any food for this trip and a discussion followed as children announced what they had brought for the journey.

Some other children joined the plane group and announced: "We're going on a Bear Hunt". Other children chimed in and the adult offered to get the book of the same

name from the outdoor shed. The boy who was the dragon found what would be the cave for the story and settled in there. The adult, plus up to five children, reenacted the story several times as the group moved actively around the garden identifying and going through the different areas named in the book. The exact details of the bear hunt changed in different retellings, guided by the children.

The example of the dragon hunt that turned into 'We're going on a Bear Hunt' highlights some key features of really good early years practice. A small group of children, mainly enthusiastic and imaginative boys, were able to develop a sustained narrative because supportive adults had provided resources and uninterrupted time. The practitioner who was most involved in this evolving narrative was very responsive to the children's ideas. She was quick to grasp and follow some sudden changes of plot, yet she also contributed her own ideas as an equal play partner with the boys. The children were able to concentrate on what most interested them at the time and readers can reflect on how individual learning was most likely extended that day – in every area of development.

Books and websites

- Community Playthings booklets and DVDs (2008) 'I made a unicorn' (2008), 'Children come first' and (2010) 'Enabling play: planning environments' (www.communityplaythings.co.uk).

- Department for Children, Schools and Families (2008, second edition) The Early Years Foundation Stage – Setting the Standards for Learning, Development and Care for children from Birth to Five, DCSF (www.teachernet.gov.uk/teachingandlearning/EYFS).

- Department for Education (2012) Statutory Framework for the Early Years Foundation Stage: Setting the Standards for Learning, Development and Care for Children from Birth to Five (www.education.gov.uk/schools/teachingandlearning/curriculum/a0068102/early-years-foundation-stage-eyfs).

- Dowling, M. (2005) *Supporting young children's sustained shared thinking: an exploration*, Early Education.

- Dowling, M. (2008) *Supporting young children's thinking through their self-chosen activities*, Early Education.

- Duckett, R., Drummond, M.J (2010) *Adventuring in early childhood education*, Sightlines Initiative.

- Early Education (2012) 'Development Matters in the Early Years Foundation Stage' (www.education.gov.uk/schools/teachingandlearning/curriculum/a0068102/early-years-foundation-stage-eyfs).

- Effective Provision of Pre-School Education Project (http://eppe.ioe.ac.uk/). This project continues to follow the original group of children into their secondary school years.

- Featherstone, S. (Ed.) (2008) *Again, Again: Understanding Schemas in Young Children*, A&C Black.

- Holland, P. (2003) *We don't play with guns here: war, weapons and superhero play in the early years*, Open University Press.

- Hope, S. (2007) *A nurturing environment for children up to three*, Islington.

- Learning and Teaching Scotland (2010) Pre-birth to three: positive outcomes for Scotland's children and families (www.ltscotland.org.uk/earlyyears/prebirthtothree/nationalguidance/index.asp).

- Lewisham Early Years Advice and Resource Network (2002) 'A place to learn: developing a stimulating environment', LEARN.

- Lindon, J. (2012) *Parents as Partners: Positive Relationships in the Early Years*, Practical Pre-School Books.

- Lindon, J. (2013) *The Key Person Approach: Positive Relationships in the Early Years*, Practical Pre-School Books.

- Lindon, J. (2012 revised edition) *Planning for Effective Early Learning*, Practical Pre-School Books.

- Lindon, J. (2011b) *Too safe for their own good? Helping children learn about risk and life skills*, National Children's Bureau.

- Lindon, J. (2012a) *What does it mean to be...? (1-4)* Series of child development books, each focusing on one year in early childhood, Practical Pre-School Books.

- Lindon, J. (2012b) *Planning for the Early Years: The local community*, Practical Pre-School Books.

- Lindon, J. (2012c) *Understanding Child Development 0-8 years*, Hodder Education.

- Lindon, J. (2012d) *Equality and Inclusion in Early Childhood*, Hodder Education.

- Lindon, J. (2012e) *Reflective Practice and Early Years Professionalism*, Hodder Education.

- Lindon, J. and Lindon, L. (2011) *Leadership and early years professionalism*, Hodder Education.

- National Strategies Early Years (2008) *Early Years Consultant's Handbook*, DCSF (https://www.education.gov.uk/schools/toolsandinitiatives/nationalstrategies).

- National Strategies Early Years (2009) *Learning, playing and interacting: Good practice in the Early Years Foundation Stage*, DCSF (https://www.education.gov.uk/schools/toolsandinitiatives/nationalstrategies).

- National Strategies Early Years (2010) *Challenging practice to further improve learning, playing and interacting in the Early Years Foundation Stage*, DCSF (https://www.education.gov.uk/schools/toolsandinitiatives/nationalstrategies)

Books and websites

- North Tyneside Children, Young People and Learning Directorate (2009) 'Enabling environments: enabling children', North Tyneside Council.

- OFSTED (2012) Conducting early years inspections (www.ofsted.gov.uk/Ofsted-home/Forms-and-guidance/Browse all by/Other/General/Conducting early years inspections).

- Rich, D. Casanova, D., Dixon, A. et al. (2005) *First hand experiences: what matters to children*, Rich Learning Opportunities (www.richlearningopportunities.co.uk).

- Rich, D. Drummond, M.J, Myer, C. (2008) *Learning: what matters to children*, Rich Learning Opportunities.

- Sightlines Initiative (2008) 'Doing the right thing: working with children in a natural environment, early childhood educators revaluate their theory and practice', Sightlines Initiative.

- Siraj-Blatchford, I., Sylva, K., Muttock, S. et al. (2002) 'Researching effective pedagogy in the early years' (www.dfes.gov.uk/research Type RB356 into the open search and you reach the summary and full report).

- Siren Films (2010) 'Two year olds outdoors – play, learning and development' and other titles (www.sirenfilms.co.uk).

- The Scottish Government (2008) Curriculum for excellence: building the curriculum 3, a framework for learning and teaching (www.ltscotland.org.uk/curriculumforexcellence/buildingthecurriculum/guidance/btc3/index.asp).

- Thornton, L., Brunton, P. (2009) *Understanding the Reggio approach: early years education in practice*, Routledge.

- Valentine, M. (2006) *The Reggio Emilia approach to early years education Learning and Teaching Scotland* (www.ltscotland.org.uk/resources/r/genericresource_tcm4242154.asp?strReferringChannel=search&strReferringPageID=tcm:4-615801-64).

- Welsh Assembly Government (2008) Framework for children's learning for 3 to 7-year-olds in Wales and Play/active learning: overview for 3 to 7-year-olds (http://wales.gov.uk/topics/educationandskills/schoolshome/curriculuminwales/arevisedcurriculumforwales/foundationphase/?lang=en).

Acknowledgements

My thanks to the managers and teams of places who made me so welcome and agreed to using examples from my visits: Garfield Children's Centre which includes the reception class of Garfield Primary School (North London), Kennet Day Nursery (Reading), Ladybirds Pre-School (Southampton), Randolph Beresford Early Years Centre (West London), Skerne Park Primary School reception class (Darlington), Start Point Sholing Early Years Centre (Southampton), Stocksfield Avenue Primary School Nursery Class (Newcastle-on-Tyne).

A huge thank you to the children in these settings, who accepted my presence and were keen to explain things to a visitor. Any children mentioned in examples have been given fictional names.

Thank you also to Robin Duckett and Emma Pace of Sightlines Initiative, Marion Dowling (early years consultant), Lisa Gadsby (early years consultant), Kathy Wesolowski and the North Tyneside early years advisory team. I learned a considerable amount during my time with the What Matters to Children team.

Notes

Notes